Grant Beck on Yeller.

**THIS BOOK IS DEDICATED TO GRANT BECK,
A REAL COWBOY,
ONE OF MY HEROES,
AND A TRUE FRIEND.**

"There's sure been a lotta good times. And the longer you live, the more often they come by. I wouldn't give a damn if I made it another year."

– Grant Beck

Grant Beck. *Photo by Dan Abernathy*

CAMP COFFEE

TALES OF A WYOMING COWBOY

BY

Bob Sullivan

ILLUSTRATIONS BY

Dan Regan

ART DIRECTION & DESIGN BY

Dusty Sumner & Jeremy Ragonese

THE LOWELL PRESS / KANSAS CITY

Sullivan House
9701 Raytown Road
Kansas City, MO
64134-2240

Manufactured in the United States of America
Printed by Greystone Graphics, Inc.
Kansas City, KS

Camp Coffee: Tales of a Wyoming Cowboy
Bob Sullivan, Jr.
1st. ed.

LCCN: 2002091612
ISBN: 0-932845-80-0
978-0-932845-80-1

1. Cowboys-Western-Wyoming

2. Sullivan, Bob, 1956- II. Title

For Sally,
Heather and Nicole,
the loves of my life.

And for the cowboy in all of us.

CONTENTS

CONTENTS

Grant Beck on Polly, a horse he broke for Ms. Tarbell at the Half Moon Ranch, Jackson, WY. This photo was taken in 1950, the year he worked for Rod Pape. He went to work full-time for the Half Moon Ranch the following year. The Grand Tetons rest in the background.

WITH HIS FACE TO THE WIND

He speaks true words and he means them,
He stands out among honorable men;
As he clings to his last shreds of freedom,
He rides out with his face to the wind.

He measures each man by his handshake,
Doesn't care for money or wealth;
He won't admit he was ever lonely,
On those nights spent alone with himself.

He's glad to share coffee and campfire,
He has no fear of death – just respect;
If he loses a stirrup at daybreak,
Hell, it was only a little wreck.

He lives in the days of his grandfather,
Wishing time could only stand still;
Knowing his fight against progress is futile,
It's like pushing a rope up a hill.

He may share his dreams in his longings,
If he can put the words in a song;
He may give her a glimpse of his loving,
Should the right woman dare come along.

He drinks whiskey that crossed Canada's border,
'Til he remembers the steps to the dance;
He'll be horseback until his last moment,
If God will just give him the chance.

He'll rise to see sunup each morning,
To ride out among other good men;
And the most he will ask from his maker,
Is a ride home with his back to the wind.

– Unknown Author

PROLOGUE

Camp Coffee is not just about a person – Grant Beck – and his stories, it's about a way of life – the cowboy way of life. Most of our children, but especially our children's children, will never feel the warmth of a high mountain camp fire or eye-burning smoke off the branding coals. The twentieth century half-heartedly embraced the legacy of the American West. Few born into this century will have any firsthand experience of what the American cowboy was all about. Lots of books have been penned about lots of cowboys, both fictitious and real. But few cowboys have touched as many people in the encouraging way that Grant Beck has through his chosen profession.

While destiny is a debatable notion, I certainly feel there was some higher order leading me to Pinedale, WY, the Two Bar Spear Ranch, and Grant Beck. For as long as I can remember I wanted to be a cowboy. Heading west from Kansas City to Wyoming in a '66 Mustang, I was fully prepared to trade-in my fuel burner for a hay burner. Throughout the course of scribing these stories, Willie Nelson's words ring as true for me now as they did the first time I heard his hit song: "I grew up dreaming of being a cowboy, and lovin' the cowboy way. Pursuing the life of my high-ridin' heroes…"

The author, age seven.

Grant Beck is one of my high-ridin' heroes in much the same way his older brother, Wells Beck, was for him. While I chose not to make a career of cowboying, I am privileged to know the man and his life and compelled to share what I learned with anyone interested in saddling up.

So much of who we evolve to be is tied into those we have known and in what we've done. If you're blessed, you can thank your parents, as I can, for providing a solid foundation. Hopefully, you all are lucky enough to have met a number of people who've made a real difference in your lives – like Grant has for me and for so many others. The distinction in the West is that the meaningful difference can come from both the two-legged and four-legged variety. And with a cowboy you can rarely separate the two.

Take the time to know Grant Beck through these stories. You'll surely appreciate what all the fuss is about. I encourage you, even though being a cowboy may never be among your career choices, to experience what it feels like in trusting your arrival to some destination on board some real horse power. It was Will Rogers who proclaimed, *"There is nothin' better for the inside of a person than the outside of a horse."* The best gift I can offer you is the affirmation that this be true.

Grant Beck and the author checking out Grant's yearling and two-year olds at the Becks' Florence, MO, farm in the fall of 2004.

Ed Wood and Donna Sievers sippin' camp coffee on a Two Bar Spear pack trip.

Chapter One

CAMP COFFEE

Camp coffee, in the literal sense, is a handful of ground coffee – more or less – thrown into an old stoneware coffee pot, no filter, just full of near-freezin', and oh-so-fresh mountain spring water. The pot is unceremoniously placed over an open campfire, or atop a wood-burning cast iron cook stove. The open fire could have been at any of a number of summer campsites in the Bridger Wilderness Area of the Wind River Range: Summit Lake, Trapper Lake, Island Lake, Gottfried or Borum Lakes. The cook stove was appropriately located in a canvas tent stretched taut over a weathered-grey timber frame. Camp was set up every fall to cater to a bevy of eager Wyoming big game hunters. This cook tent was nestled in a mixed grove of Aspen and Pine trees in a breath-taking setting, situated to the north of Jackson Hole, WY – below Sheep Mountain, just above the Gros Ventre River. This picturesque spot is located where the Teton National Park and Teton National Forest converge. It offers such spectacular views and serene ambience, one was often tempted to never leave camp.

Wherever the camp coffee was percolatin', you'd find Grant Beck. You didn't get Grant without his collection of yarns and tales. It was always a difficult task to tell which was more flavorful, the coffee or the stories. On a cold mountain morning the steamin' cup of coffee warmed your hands while Grant's stories warmed your heart. Grant's tales are genuine, told from his heart. They convey the true spirit of the West – few of us can imagine, and all of us envy.

From a personal perspective "camp coffee" was reflective in crawling from my goose down Northface bag to an early, pre-dawn frost. Inhaling mountain air so fresh and full of life it finds one's core. A high country scent too natural to take for granted. The first conscious breath triggered an overwhelming eagerness for the first glimmer of morning sun to unmask the beauty of the surrounding environs. It was the fall of 1976. Every morning provided me an euphoric rush. I'd been hired on by Grant to help with the wrangling, guiding, and cooking - catering to the whims of that season's hunters. I couldn't imagine a place more deserving of an artist's canvas than those views from hunting camp up in the Gros Ventre. How fortuitous it was for Grant and me to have crossed paths that previous July during Pinedale's annual Green River Rendezvous pageant. Hunting camp in Wyoming's high county was a far departure from the town of Pinedale and the Cowboy Bar. We had a shot and a beer. We toasted working together and the coming fall.

After shaking out the cobwebs by splashing ice-cold mountain water from the nearby mountain stream on my face each morning, I returned to the inviting warmth of the cook tent, where the camp coffee had just started to boil. But it wasn't quite camp coffee yet. No, camp coffee is not complete until an always-uneven pour of Jack Daniels was added to the steaming brew, both of ours, and sipped during the newest adaptation from Grant's wealth of western experiences. That's the recipe. All three ingredients – the steaming coffee, Jack Daniels, and the stories – are required. That's how each and every morning started in hunting camp, Grant, Jack and I. If one was truly fortunate there was a second cup and one last tale before it was time to roust the hunters and wrangle the horses.

The Grand Tetons from above hunting camp.

Chapter Two

ON THE WAY

KIDS TURN OUT

Grant Beck has always been a philosopher of sorts. Call it his views of the West. He offers an opinion about everything from Osama Bin Laden to the proper knot in tying a lead-line to a fence post. His opinions are from a perspective based partly on his personal life, but mostly on his dealings with other folks' lives. Grant's experiences center on horses and people. He can read people the same uncanny way he can read a horse. You look at 'em; watch how they hold their heads, their posture, look into their eyes. Especially take note on how they look back at you. Study their behavior and you'll learn something about what makes them tick. Grant values a good horse and a good person on much the same par. He shares his opinion of their value with anyone interested in listening. He has no tolerance for a second-class horse, and less tolerance for a second-class individual. In his mind the only difference between the two is how you get rid of 'em.

"You can't send a human to a glue factory or tie 'em to a tree as bear-bait."

Things are much less complicated with a horse. In Grant's world life is too short to spend time fussin' with either.

In reflecting back on his contributions, nothing has ever been more important to him than the kids he has shared time with at his summer camps over the past half century since 1957. Grant has made a difference in each of their lives. A positive one? You bet. It was true for me. I've seen how it has helped make my eldest daughter a lot more independent. Of course, Grant never takes credit for the

Grant Beck and Miller Wood at the Two Bar Spear Ranch in the summer of 1989.

way anyone turns out, even when it's obvious he's made a difference. He does have an opinion on what the most significant influence on a young person's life is:

> *"Everything will go back home, one way or another. Back to where it started. That's just the way life is. I've been watchin' my own family. Ten years after we lost both our parents, I was the only one kept askin' questions and goin' to see neighbors who knew the folks.*
>
> *Used to go to the cemetery with dad in the buggy. We'd take plants grown in the house, you know? Mother always had flowers a growin'. We'd take one of those, make a hole, shake it out of the container, and plant it. We'd just go once a year to the cemetery and clean the weeds out. Now it's a beautiful cemetery in Rigby, ID."*

Little by little, one plant at a time, Grant provided his kin with a beautiful resting place. The sum of the parts made the whole. Just as it is his belief how each of us are about the aggregate of our youthful experiences. As adults, our behavior reflects our parents' upbringing. It has been paraphrased to me as "the apple don't fall too far from the tree."

Grant Beck sharing some of his horse wisdom with Two Bar Spear campers, class of '89. The author's daughter Heather is seated to Grant's right.

Chapter Three

NOT A TELEVISION COWBOY

"My brother, Lamar Beck, he went to school with the guy who invented television – Philo T. Farnsworth. He had a lot of ability and smarts. He moved to Rigby, ID. When he was 14 - years-old, he showed his invention to my sister and my two brothers. One of them, Wells, didn't give a damn about anything but a horse."

Philo Taylor Farnsworth was born in 1906 near Beaver Creek, UT. He and his family moved to a ranch in Rigby, ID, population 2,500, when he was 12. Like the Beck kids, Philo relied on a horse to transport him back and forth the four miles to and from high school every day. But his interest was never in farming or ranching but in electricity, although it is said that his idea for the television came "while looking at long rows he had just plowed on his family farm. His thought was to scan an optical image row after row from left to right, which would be converted into an electron image."

"Philo took 'em down in his cellar and he showed 'em how he could get a picture. It come through a little old tiny delta light plant run by a gas motor. Philo could touch these wires together and he had kind of a window with the wires across it. He could show lines on it like you see on television. Ya' know when you can't get nothin'. He got that from a delco light plant. It took the Russian – Vladimir Zworykin, employed by RCA, applied for a patent on Farnsworth's transmitter in 1923 – less than a week to get a patent on it."

Grant Beck in his early years, about 1934, at the age of eight.

Philo Farnsworth did indeed invent the television although credit was not immediately forthcoming. The quick chronology is this:

1921: Philo Farnsworth has an idea for how to create images using electrons.
1927: He transmits the first electronic image.
1934: Farnsworth stages the first demonstration of his TV system.
1935: The U.S. Patent office awards to Farnsworth a "priority of invention."
1939: Following seven years of litigation with RCA over who actually invented television, Philo Farnsworth finally receives his just recognition and starts collecting royalties from RCA.

Other than living in the same town and attending the same high school – Grant for just one year; he dropped out, moved to Daniel, WY, to embark on his life as a cowboy. Philo for just two, he gained admission into Brigham Young University at age 15 – the thing the two had most in common was their perceived value of Philo's invention. Grant has never had a TV in his main cabin or guest cabins at the Two Bar Spear Ranch. Grant figured the value of what he had to offer was outdoors and not in. Philo's attitude toward his invention was much more cynical. He felt he had created a kind of monster. He'd invented a way for people to waste a good portion of their lives. Philo's son Kent was once quoted, "Throughout my childhood his dad's reaction to television was, 'There's nothing on it worthwhile, and we're not going to watch it in this household, and I don't want it in your intellectual diet'." I wonder what Philo would think if he spent a day in front of it today?

Philo Farnsworth and the Beck children had one other thing in common, a teacher, Justin Tolman, who had a significant effect on the direction of their lives.

> *"All six of us kids and Philo had the same teacher sometime in our life. I was the last one – the youngest. Justin Tolman, he advised me to quit school."*

Justin Tolman is also credited with recognizing and encouraging Philo Farnsworth's genius. Farnsworth both formally and publicly credited Tolman with providing him with inspiration and essential knowledge.

Chapter Four

$5 AND A CHANGE OF CLOTHES

"I had just started my freshman year. I quit school in October and worked in a sugar factory until it closed down. They always hired kids to oil up high where you had to climb and I got a job as an oiler at the elevator at the sugar factory. The factory was located halfway between Rigby and Idaho Falls. People had worked there for 20 years, always at the same job. We had a couple of neighbors who worked there and I got a ride with them. It was on their shift that the plant needed an oiler. Hell, I did pretty good. I was makin' 40 cents an hour. Haulin' manure or somethin' with a team, you might get a dollar and your dinner each day. That was big money!

When the sugar beet run was over, and the plant closed, I went to Nevada with a sheep shearin' crew. Left with them the first of February. I was tyin' fleeces. Got a penny a fleece and my board. All I needed to do was furnish my sleeping bag and clothes. I could tie 1,000 a day, so I was makin' ten bucks a day. I was always the only one in camp who had any money. We'd move from one job to the next. This contractor I was workin' for would give me money every week for the last job. Well, once in town, these shearers would drink and gamble and eventually run out of money. They'd spend all of theirs then end up spendin' all mine too. When I left that job I had $5.00 in my pocket but new clothes inside and out. I didn't even bring my sleeping bag home it was so filthy. Damn sheep fleece, oil in it you know? So I went home with my five dollars. Didn't know what I was goin' to do. I went down to the drugstore in Rigby to see when the bus come in. Thought, I guess I'll get on it, and go to Pinedale."

Pinedale is about 80 miles southeast of Jackson, WY. Jackson is on the other side of Teton Pass from Rigby, ID. Grant decided on Pinedale because his older brother Wells had worked for ranchers in that area for the past few years. Grant had helped him rake hay there one summer, so he had some familiarity with Pinedale. Plus, he had a connection. I suppose for a 14-year-old, who was pretty much on his own, the 'connection' weighed-in pretty significantly. Grant took a bus to Victor, ID. Victor was at the bottom of Teton Pass on the west side, but Grant needed to get to Jackson, WY, at the bottom of the pass on the east side. Grant would somehow need to conjure up a ride.

Raking and piling hay, as practiced during the time of this story, at the Campbell's Ranch in Bondurant, WY.

"The bus give me a ride to Victor, ID, just the other side of Teton Pass. And I walked to the top of the son-of-a-bitch. I finally got a ride down. I was pretty little then, didn't start to grow 'til I come to Wyoming. I was short but I grew like a weed the first summer. It was just good eatin' and plenty of exercise. About every curve he'd say, 'But ought you not to be in school?' That was the fifth of April. When we got to Jackson he pulled up to the sheriff's office. While he was in the sheriff's office I got out. There was a hotel there, but it's a gift store now. It was on the road up from the hospital, on the last turn before you turned around the square, on the

right side. It looked like the cheapest place to get a room. I only had $2.50 left. The bus ticket had cost me $2.50. I had everything I owned in one of those satchels. When commercial airplanes first came out, they called 'em airplane duffel bags. They were waterproof. I had one change of clothes. So I went to this hotel and asked the lady if she had a room. She said yes, it would be $2.50. That was going to leave me broke so I'd have to hitchhike to Pinedale. She asked me where I was goin'. I told her Pinedale. She asked me if I knew the Richardson family in Daniel just west of Pinedale. I said yeah, my brother's worked for them for about five years, and I was goin' to get on with them."

"I went to Daniel when I left Jackson. When the lady at the hotel found out I was goin' to the Richardson Place she said that they were one of her best friends. She wouldn't take a nickel from me. She gave me the best supper, and a good bed, and told me if I wanted to shower, she had a good shower, and I was welcome to it. Next mornin' she drove me to the bus depot. The bus ticket to Daniel was $2.50. So I got on the bus. Well, a fellow by the name of Don Querey had the contract for the bus. When I went to get off I asked him what I owed him. He replied, 'Why don't you wait until you get to workin' and you can leave the bus fare with Dick Key.' Dick ran the store at Daniel junction. Austin Richardson picked me up. Before I headed to the ranch, I left the $2.50 there at the store for that bus ride. Don, he never picked it up. About the middle of July I was in the store and Dick Key said, 'Don don't want your money, no need of me hangin' on to it.' He gave it back to me. I never saw that bus driver again. Not for about six years, when I was 20, and I was surprised as hell when I did. I was shoein' horses for the Half Moon Ranch in Moose, WY, just north of Jackson. He hauled in our camp kids, the Half Moon kids, over from the Victor, ID, train station, over the mountain in his bus. He opened the doors. I was shoein' horses from about here to the cow barn, to where he had to pull-up to turn around. He pulled in there, opened the doors, and let the kids get their duffels out. He came over to where I was shoein', and said, 'Well, I've seen you somewhere before.' When I'd seen it was him, I stood up and shook his hands, and he gave me the best hug I ever had in my life. He said, 'I don't know why, but I just knew you'd amount to something'."

Don hauled the kids to the Half Moon Ranch each of the seven years Grant worked there. The Half Moon Ranch was owned by Anita Tarbell. She hailed from Boston, MA, and was one of the handful of enterprising and tough-spirited East Coast folks that were drawn, early on, by the allure of Jackson Hole and the Tetons. The attraction was enough to inspire them to take up seasonal residence there and start dude ranches so that East Coast kids could have a Western experience. Grant met his first wife, Eleanor, at the Half Moon. They were married in 1953 at the famous Church of the Transfiguration at Moose Junction, right across the river from the Half Moon. The ceremony was held on the 29th of June. All of the flowers in the church had been gathered growing wild in the Tetons. The Half Moon's campers that year went up and picked them the day before the wedding. Miss Tarbell, as she was affectionately referred to by Grant, hosted the reception at the Half Moon. I never had the pleasure of meeting Eleanor. Things did not work out between her and Grant. The reason in Grant's own words,

> *"It was not a mistake marryin' that gal. She was good. I just didn't plan on marryin' the whole family."*

Church of the Transfiguration at Moose Junction, WY.

Wells Beck, about 1930.

Chapter Five

MY HEROES HAVE ALWAYS BEEN COWBOYS

"Wells was on me constantly. He was like to kill me. He was gonna make a hand out of me in one season."

Wells Beck was the first of Grant's siblings to choose the life of a cowboy. Grant was nine when his dad died. Wells was 23. For most of us growing up, our dad is one of our heroes – one of the people we want to be like when we grow up. When it comes to heroes other than our dads, choices often are based upon characters seen on TV or at the movies. This is typically the case if our heroes happen to be cowboys.

For Grant, Wells became all of these things: a father figure, a hero, and the cowboy Grant wanted to be. One can only imagine the pressure Wells felt being put up on a pedestal by a kid brother. Under that type of pressure, mistakes are made. Wells wasn't perfect. Even when acting or living in a manner less than admirable, he still set an example for Grant. Grant grew up watching and learning from Wells, both the good and the bad. Where Wells failed in Grant's eyes, Grant made a conscious effort to be different – to be better – whether on how to treat a horse or how to treat a person. After all, when Grant was 13, there was no TV to perpetuate a cowboy role model - only the real deal.

For all their similarities, Wells and Grant were different; most often though, they cowboyed on the same spread. Comparisons of the two were often drawn by those who employed them. Mildred Miller is the matriarch of one of Sublette County's great ranching families. The Circle Ranch with its 67 brand has been around for four or five generations. Grant lost his mother at the same young age he lost his father. Of the women who have been most influential in Grant's life, helping fill that maternal void, most noticeably was his sister Loretta. Grant holds nothing but the fondest memories of his older sister who struggled emotionally when Grant left home for Wyoming at 13-years-of-age. At the top of the list of the other women who played a significant role in Grant's upbringing is Mildred Miller.

"There were two or three of the ranchers around Daniel I'd met the previous summer: the Scott Place that is now owned by Philips Petroleum and the Richardson's. I got to go and help Wells rake hay the summer before I went to Nevada with the shearing crew. That's when I really got to like it!

The Scott Place, they run about 500 cows at that time. Now the Millers have it, and they run a couple thousand head there, I bet. The Miller Ranch is all divided up now since Bobby Miller passed on. Bobby had four kids: Mike from his first marriage; Matt and twin sisters from his second marriage. Mike's mother is great. Mike's 50-years old. He was the rookie bronc rider of the year, one year. He makes a ton of money trainin' horses. He sells a lot of horses for $30, $40 thousand. He will be the biggest Miller land owner when it's all said and done. He's into reinin' and cuttin' horses, and owns an own son of Colonel Freckles. Got him through artificial insemination. Mike's just a fine guy.

Bobby was runnin' the ranch when you were at the Two Bar Spear. I had gone down there that spring and helped him castrate and brand their colts. I had Eagle, my Triple Chick stud, then. And Mildred, Mike's mother, heard that I had a Triple Chick colt. She came out when we were about done brandin' and told me to go out to the corral and pick out two mares to breed to that fine colt of mine. She give 'em to me. Mildred treated me really good all the time. I worked for them quite a bit."

Bob Beard was a foreman at The Circle Ranch. There's a story recalled by Bob about one of the Beck boys who "used to rope calves and tie hard and fast. He never let go of the rope. And the rope happened to get caught up under the tail of his horse. Well, his horse got to buckin', and by the time the rodeo was over he cleared out the whole branding corral." Afterwards Bob took him aside and had a long talk with him. Mildred quickly replied upon hearing this story, "that must've been Wells Beck, not Grant."

Wells tended to be more brash than Grant, both with horses and people. He had a bit of an ornery streak when it came to his relationships. Grant was always aware of Wells' harshness. He made a promise to himself not to emulate that trait. Mildred Miller, as well as everyone else who knew both Becks, recognized this difference in the brothers. Both were top hands and sought after by all the area ranches. When Grant first moved to Daniel he searched out Wells, and for years followed him from ranch to ranch.

He watched, listened and learned in his quest to hone his cowboy skills.

"Wells was on me constantly. He was like to kill me. He was gonna make a hand out of me in one season. Christ, he'd work an unbroken horse, ride it half mile down the road and back then give it to me to rake hay with. Naturally, I was kinda concerned about it. So I was plum awake. I was ahead of the horse all the time. And I never had no problem. Pretty quick, why he was puttin' them teams together after four drivings. I was rakin' with two colts. I made out with that. He was pretty tough to get along with, especially when he seen he wasn't causin' me to have a wreck; scared the hell out of me! I had one runaway. He told me at the beginnin' of the season, if you have a runaway and lose your team, you might as well follow them horses cuz you're fired anyway.

Wells Beck in high country.

We was tryin' to finish up hayin' and I was scatter-rakin', following the sweeps ya know, pickin' up behind them. Drivin' in a trot. It was a rough meadow. All at once my damn doubletree pin jumped out. We had rakes with trucks on 'em: two little carts in front where you could turn square around and not hit your wheels. It was really the best way to go. Well, when the doubletree pin come out, the neck yoke come off, and I had a hold of the team, and I landed ahead of the truck. I drug around on my belly out there, and held on to them damn things with just a doubletree and finally they quit runnin'. I drove them up to the stack yards. Wells was up there stackin' hay and laughin' at me. When he got down, I was madder than hell. I was really mad, and I said, 'Why you son-of-a-bitch you think that was funny, didn't ya? Damn you. Find someone else to drive 'em. I've had all I want of you and that team, too.' That's the only time I ever stood up to him. 'Oh calm down,' he said. I said, 'Well you drive 'em cuz they're all yours'."

"I started off. Hell, I was a mile and half from the ranch. I started walking up the road. It was damn near quittin' time. He was pushin' everybody to try to hurry cuz there was a cloud comin' in and usually there'd be a little rain - enough to stop you. I guess it was about five o'clock. They caught up to me with the wagon. We went back and forth, hollerin' and arguin' with one another in the wagon. Wells had the team tied on behind and the stacker team pullin' the wagon. So I got in and rode on up there. I went in and told Beth and Austin Richardson that I've had all I want workin' around Wells. Runaway or not, I've had all I want.

'Wells is an awful hard worker and sometimes he works too hard and he's too tired and he don't think what he says,' that was Austin talking. He was a great guy. 'Well I think I'll leave in the morning.' 'You just wait the night,' Austin said. The next mornin' Wells is a different person. He must've talked until 10:30 the night before with Austin. He went through everything, how he'd rode me all summer, and Austin told 'em you can't grow that boy up that fast. That's what he told 'em. So, I stayed on.

Wells did some great things there. He wasn't all bad. He was just hard for me to get along with. We was just too much alike. He just had an ornerier streak around horses than I did. I was gettin' a little further along with one easier than he was. I don't know if it showed up then or not but I'm sure that was the problem. I could get on a colt that he give me to break. I'd ride around the round corral, get off, pick up its feet and play with 'em. He didn't have time for that. When he got one goin' around the corral in a walk, he'd go from that to a gallop. He had a hackamore and tried to rough stop it. Hell, I'd stop a young horse in training in two or three steps. Then I'd change to a snaffle bit. Oh Wells, he'd bellyache about that. According to Wells, that wasn't the way to start one. Christ, he didn't know nothin' about it 'til he come to Wyoming. Hell, we never had that many colts back home in Idaho, mostly work draft horses where we grew-up."

Grant's memories of Wells contain equal amounts of fondness and bitterness. As I look back over the years I've known Grant, and through all of the stories I've heard, I know two things: Grant turned out to be one helluva a hand, and he helped a great many folks be better at whatever they chose for themselves in life. In Grant's heart there is a place proudly reserved for the role that Wells played in the scheme of things.

Wells Beck at the Half Moon Ranch, 1950.

Chapter Six

MILDRED, BETH AND MARIE

"Everybody I worked for wanted to put me back in school, except for Mildred Miller. She was like a second mother to me. Beth and Austin were gonna put me in school, they already put me in 4-H. They give me a calf to use for 4-H. My calf led good and all that stuff and was really a good lookin' calf. Austin picked it out for me. He let the cat-out-of-the-bag tellin' me what nice school clothes that calf would bring when we sell him at the fair - the county auction. I give the calf back to him and I told him, 'you better butcher that calf cuz I don't need it.'

I quit once or twice there just becuz they tried to get close to puttin' me in school, just before we started hayin'. One time I quit and I jumped the fence and went over to work for John and Marie Meyers. Ol' Marie and Beth, they had better track of me than I did myself. I'd cry on Marie's shoulder and she'd tell Beth what I had to say. Austin would come over and say, 'I can't get anyone to milk these cows decent like you do. Just come milk the cows. If you don't want to work in the hay field then that's all right.'

They really politicked me around I thought. They were good to me. When Austin had a heart attack up in the Basin huntin' elk and died, Beth sold the ranch and she moved to San Antonio. She had a sister who had a school for gifted children, and Beth went down there to help her and stayed there until she died. I moved her down to San Antonio with a U-Haul trailer. It was really a fun trip. I drove her car and then took the bus back home. When Beth died, she willed me $37,000. She willed another lady up in Daniel $37,000. That lady kept hers and I turned mine back. Told 'em to give it to Austin, Jr., their adopted kid. I sent it back to the trust.

Beth was really a good lady. Her and Austin married after she was too old to have children. I think they was both 48 when they got married. They put their name in at The Cradle, or whatever the orphanage was called in Chicago. Their adoption request had been there three years. They didn't get a baby. I think they was over 50 when they got the baby. And they got Austin, and he was brain-damaged then. I could tell it in him when I went there. He wanted to ride around with me irrigatin' or haulin' hay, whatever I was doin'.

He tagged around a lot. But they had him tutored all the time. And when he was three, well they adopted a little girl; she was fine. And, she was almost two, walkin' good, and the kids were playin' outside where there was some puddles. Beth had her dressed up in a snow suit, stompin' around in the puddles, and she fell down on her stomach in a puddle and drowned. Austin kept on a playin'. Finally he went to the house and said, 'Mary Caroline, she won't get up.' Beth went out and found her.

They had relatives cuz Austin had a sister that lived up Horsecreek, the head of Horsecreek. The damn snow was as high as the fence post. Wells came in from feedin'. He always had a saddle horse to feed with. He rode that horse up there, about 14 miles, and told the Thompson family about this little girl dyin'. They got back about 2:30 in the morning. He said all he could go by to get his bearings was a fence post every once in a while, because his tracks blew in with snow on the way up there.

To come here like I did and see the opportunities open to me was somethin'. But it was people like Mildred Miller, Beth Richardson, and Marie Meyers – the way those three ladies looked after me makes me wanna cry rememberin' it."

Chapter Seven

OL' COWBOY

"I believe my best horse ever was 'Ol' Cowboy'."

Grant Beck's owned so many good horses it's hard to imagine how he could pick out just one. Everyone who's worked for him, or spent time at the ranch, has had a favorite. I've ridden several of his horses through the years and they've all been good. Each one different and evoking its own unique personality. I certainly can't pick out a favorite. For Abie Beck, Grant's wife for the past 22 years, it is definitely Amigo.

Abigail Dowd journeyed west from Charlotte, NC, in 1979, having signed on as a counselor for the Two Bar Spear summer camp. Some 30 years Grant's junior, no one suspected that they would one day end up bound in the harmony of marriage. It seemed right when it happened, the following year in 1982; and still seems right today.

Grant Beck on Cowboy, 1958.

For some of Grant's counselors the most dependable horse was Taylor Maid, Amigo, Arial, or even Ironwood. At 19, when I first met Grant, I bought a three-year old gelding named Bud from him. He was pretty special. I can't imagine a better horse for hunting camp than King. During hunting camp in 1976 King was my first choice whenever Grant wasn't riding him back. A lot of people rode King and loved him. In fact, he ended up on Big Richie Proveromo's ranch in Fairplay, CO, after Grant retired him from ranch service. Richie had owned Tillie's Saloon in Breckenridge, CO, for years. Later, while Richie owned him, King posed for a Land's End catalogue ad.

But back to Cowboy:

"Cowboy come off of Austin Richardson's ranch. I was about 16 when I got him. First he give 'em to my brother – Wells. He'd broke a lot of horses for Austin. Wells, he didn't think he had any use for Cowboy, so I got him. I took him to Jackson. I had him over there in the rodeo. I roped off him. And I broke a few horses over there with him. I snubbed un-broke horses for other people. He was a horse like this big gray out in the field. There ain't nothin' you can't do on 'em."

Grant Beck halter breaking a colt at the Richardson Place in the mid-to-late 1940s.

Snubbing a horse is tying a young or unbroke horse, by the lead line from its halter, to the saddle horn of a mature, broke horse. This ensures that the young horse is held close and under control while a rider climbs aboard. This practice is often used in the early training process of two-to-three-year-old horses in order to safely ride them around a breaking pen or corral.

"I had my saddle on the big gray. I forgot to tighten the cinch. The saddle had fallen clear down here, on his side. The horse I had snubbed to him still hangin' back. Had me pinned to where I couldn't get out. Finally that colt runs ahead, and when he did, I just stepped off the other side. The other leg was free anyway. I fell right down underneath him. The gray horse never flinched. I got up and un-cinched him and straightened up the saddle, before I ever thought to see where the other horse was. He was still dallied around the horn and the rope was crossed. Christ, he'd of kicked my saddle all to hell if he'd jerked at all. I got up and got it cinched up and back on. That's the type of horse ol' Cowboy was.

Like ol' Cowboy, he's automatic. Same way cuttin' cattle. If you sit on as many horses as I have in a lifetime, there were several that coulda made champion horses. Cuttin', ropin', chariot racin', whatever. They had the disposition and quality to do that type of stuff. But that didn't pay near as much as goin' up the trail with a guest on 'em. That's the only way I seen that I could buy the Two Bar Spear Ranch and operate summer and huntin' camps. Buyin' the ranch and runnin' the summer camp, pack trips, and hunting camp – that's the best thing I ever done."

Grant Beck on his Harley, about 1952.

Chapter Eight

NOT A HAY BURNER

If you looked up cowboy or horseman in a dictionary of the West and found a picture of Grant Beck, there could be no argument. If Grant was depicted on a horseback in that same listing it would be expected. Envision the consummate horseman. A cowboy sitting in a saddle so naturally, so comfortably, one can't distinguish where the man ends and the horse begins. But even Grant found the occasional thrill in a different kind of saddle. It's tough to imagine but there was a time when Grant could be found straddling a "Harley," as in Harley-Davidson.

Like horses, motorcycles too offer their special breeds. When choosing his four-legged mounts, Grant went for the ride that always delivered the best performance. Not surprisingly, his mount was always a good looker too. So when Grant decided there was the need to get from point A to point B just a tad quicker than horseback, he headed to a Harley dealer across the Wyoming state line into Montana. It was there Grant picked out his mechanical steed. A wild-eyed and bit unkempt 14-year-old enthusiast, who introduced himself as Bobby, furnished Grant with his first two-wheel driving lesson. His hair might have been lonesome for a comb, but this kid boarded a motorcycle about as easily as you might slide into some well-worn slippers. Grant wasn't the least bit surprised how much at ease Bobby handled the bikes. Somehow though, the riggin' on this gas-propelled two-wheeler didn't quite accommodate Grant's spurs.

> *"It was the first time I ever rode a motorcycle. This young kid was rarin' to show me how it was done. He grabbed hold of one of them motor bikes and had it spittin' up gravel and dust in no time. As much as there was nothin' I thought I couldn't do on a horse, it seemed much the same for him on a motorcycle. He went through his demonstration so quickly, I'd been embarrassed to ask him to show me agin. Reckon this was about all the learnin' I was gonna get. It looked 'bout fun enough to get me to try it. Damned if I didn't drive away with one."*

It wasn't until many years later that Grant put together who'd given him his inaugural motorcycle lesson. Of course, by that time the boy had grown up. He'd also changed his name to Evel.

Robert Craig Knievel was born in the copper mining town of Butte, MT, on Oct. 17, 1938. He was 12 years Grant's junior. Like Grant's father, Bob Knievel had spent time working in a mineshaft. He'd also briefly operated a hunting guide service in Montana. Prior to becoming the world's most famous motorcycle rider and daredevil, and picking up the "Evel" nickname, Knievel had served in the army, sold insurance, and even robbed a few banks.

Where Grant chose horses as his passion, Knievel chose motorcycles. Swap the grease stains for the soiled marks where Grant's jeans rubbed his saddle and the twos' spirits were almost identical. The main difference between them is that their careers are polar opposites relative to the public domain. Evel's exploits are known the world over, his name practically a household word. Grant's contributions have always been private. He never asked for his life to be published. The positive influence Grant has had on young people through sharing his way of life never was worn on his shirtsleeve.

Grant Beck posing with his mechanical steed.

Grant Beck on Grady.

Chapter Nine

GRADY

"Grady was a real good rope horse, and he was gentle for everybody."

There are few things that Grant Beck enjoys talking about more than his horses. And he's had a lot of 'em. So many in fact, that every time he is describing the traits in one, a dozen more comes to mind. No individual horse story is ever finished. For Grant, it's like a mother talking about her children. If you talk about one too much, you're guilty in not giving the rest equal bragging time.

I've attempted on several occasions to get Grant to pick his favorite horse. Each time he starts and ends the stories with a different horse. There are certain ones that always come up. At the same time, a horse he hasn't mentioned before often surfaces from his wonderful collection of memories. For most of us horse lovers, having one horse of the caliber of Grant's many "favorites" would be enough. One never tires of seeing the sparkle in Grant's eyes when he's telling of them. But the stories don't always end up being just about the horses.

Grant and I were enjoying a cup of camp coffee and each other's company. Instead of sitting around the campfire, we were at the kitchen table in his Florence, MO, farm house. I'd asked him how he came by Grady.

> *"Boyd Kelly, that's where Grady'd come from. Grady'd been trained by Toots Mansfield, World Champion Roper. They built a saddle that Toots'd showed them would be a good one to rope in. That saddle is still on the market. Toots was a helluva good roper - one of the leading ropers of his time. Boyd sold his ranch and went to Los Angeles. Later he moved to Reno where he bought a bar and liquor store. He'd had a helluva big ranch in Daniel, WY.*

I'd been workin' for the Millers. I got mad at 'em. Everybody went to town on a Saturday night and got drunk but me. We had a huge herd of cattle at the Flyin' V. The Flyin' V was located just before you get to Daniel, on the right side. We had to trail the cattle to Big Piney, and had to sort-off about 300 cows that'd lost their calves and were dry. We had to sort some pairs off too. Everybody out there workin' these cattle was drunk and hung over but me. Bob Miller, he'd single me out no matter where I was at, and he'd holler, 'Get over here and help me Grant!'

He'd had two or three of them hands. My brother Wells and the others about that same age, laughin' and carryin' on. They didn't give a shit about nothin'. Bob hollered at me about three times, and finally I just rode into the middle of the herd, and I said, 'you can just stick this frickin' place any where you want.' I just rode off the Flyin' V and turned my horse loose.

So I quit Millers' and went to work for Boyd Kelly. He'd been married to Pat about a year. Boyd been married before and had one daughter. Hell, his new wife, Pat, she was younger than me. And his first wife was about five years older. Boyd he was 55 or so. I was feedin' cattle at his ranch, me and another guy. There was this third guy, can't remember his name, feedin' up on Horse Creek. All three of us was pitchin' hay. Me and Earl was rakin' hay

Feeding hay in a Wyoming winter, ca. 1950.

for Boyd, and breakin' some colts. Kept us in saddle horses. Kelly'd went to the Denver Stock Show, him and Pat. They was down in Denver one day when a neighbor, Delbert Ball, from up at Horse Creek, called him. 'You might want to send your man some help up here,' Delbert says, 'he gets a load of hay one day and feeds it all the next. Not many willows left on the crick to boot, cattle chewed 'em all down. He just about run 'em clean up.' Delbert was a helluva good friend to everybody.

So Boyd, he'd called Delbert, and Earl answered the phone. Boyd told Earl he wanted to talk to me. I went over to the phone, and Boyd says, 'kid can you take a couple of saddle horses and go up to the Craner place and find out where all that hay is goin? Just send that guy down. Think you can do that?' I said, 'No, only way I can do that is take the four head of horses I been workin' all winter. I broke two of them. And you know damn well if he wasn't feedin' them cows, he weren't feedin' the horses neither. 'And he wasn't feedin' 'em. He'd been jabbin' 'em horses with a pitch fork and shit like that. One horse he poked, hell I had to borrow penicillin from the Millers to doctor it.

Bob Miller, he'd had six hay-diggers up there and they had 700 cows. There was seven hay-diggers and a cook until I'd quit 'em. At the Craner place feedin' for Boyd, I had 340 head of cows that I was feedin' by myself. So naturally I'd be a tad bit late for dinner. Hell that didn't matter. Ol' Pete, who cooked for Boyd, he didn't care, he always cooked a lot. Boyd and Pat come back from Denver. I'd heard they were back through the mail lady, Mrs. David.

Mrs. David took the mail up two days a week from Murlin down to Pinedale. She come back and hung the mail sack on the road as I went by. The only mail me or the rest of them ever got was cigarettes and stuff from the store. But Boyd, he'd sent this letter up, for me to come down to the ranch. So I come down. I went to get cleaned-up first. I'd wore-out half my clothes that I'd took up there with me. Didn't have none too many anyway. Oh it'd take two hours to ride from the Craner place to Horse Creek. They had a good sleigh at the Craner place. There was a snow road all the way to Horse Creek, where it crossed the Green River. That's where Steve James is trainin' horses today – same ranch he's on.

Boyd just wanted to know how I was gettin' along. We all went in town for supper. Boyd bought a room in the hotel. I give out on 'em about nine o'clock. He give me the keys to his room. 'When we get ready to go,' Boyd said, 'I'll come and get you.' He come up about two a.m., said, 'we're goin' to stay with the Johnson's tonight.' They're the ones that had the bar. Boyd said, 'I'll see ya in the mornin. Just go down and get whatever you want to eat and drink.' He told me that I was goin' to be boardin' here a day or so.

'I'm goin' to stay, hell. If you think I'm gonna go back the second time to a hungry bunch of cows you're crazy!' 'They're all right,' Boyd said.

Boyd and Pat went up to the Craner place and stayed about two weeks. Boyd seen that I had everything under control, and they left. When they'd come up, I was feedin' hay over at Lester Pape's. I was drivin' cattle from Boyd's place to Lester Pape's. I fed the hay to Boyd's cattle there. Then I moved to Barrows' place where I fed 700 cows, and 85 head of yearling and two-year-old horses. Barrows come-out and helped me. Boyd, he'd helped me too. I give somebody my horse and I got them cattle out of the field. I just took the team and sleigh and led 'em out with a load of hay when we got 'em moved over to Barrows' from Pape's. I was board and roomin' with the Bar Cross crew while I was up there.

When Boyd come up there to help, why he'd given me an envelope. He said, 'I got your check here.' But he'd already mailed me a check. He'd had Pat make me a second one. They would usually pay me one on the first and one on the 15th. They wouldn't take neither envelope back. When I opened the second envelope they give me, in addition to a second check, there was the bill of sale to a sorrel horse – a good son-of-a-gun.

I had to drive to Rock Springs and get the horse off of the railroad. He'd been shipped out from California. They'd shipped him out there from Boyd's ranch to get him broke. He'd originally come to Boyd's from the Haythorn Ranch in Nebraska. That's were he was foaled. He was out of a pretty good stud – a quarter horse stud they'd called Old Sorrel. Old Sorrel's sire was Hickory Bill. I had his full pedigree.

Boyd, he'd bought four head at the Denver Stock Show, and he'd give me that horse as a bonus. Grady was all broke and trained in California by a professional, Toots Mansfield. I'd worked for Boyd a year, I guess, after I worked for the Millers. And that's where Grady'd come from."

Haythorn Land & Cattle is a fifth-generation ranching family who raises cattle and horses on 90,000 acres in the Nebraska Sand Hills. The ranch headquarters are in Arthur, NE, located about 17 miles north of Ogallala. They were the first ranch to register Quarter Horses in the state of Nebraska. Haythorn Land & Cattle is the third largest breeder of Quarter Horses in the world.

Old Sorrel was a foundation Quarter Horse standing stud on the King Ranch of Texas. He was foaled in 1915 and died on the ranch in 1946. A good many performance Quarter Horses can be traced back to his pedigree. If Grant's recollection is accurate, Grady truly was from well-respected foundation stock.

The Half Moon Ranch, ca. 1950.

Chapter Ten

THE HALF MOON RANCH

"Half Moon Ranch boys and girls keep showin' up here. Their experiences at the ranch had a lasting effect on their lives."

– Doris Platts, April 2002

Doris Platts was a Half Moon Ranch counselor from 1959 through 1966, and now resides in Wilson, WY.

The spectacular beauty of the Grand Tetons towering majestically over the picturesque valley surrounding Jackson Hole captured the attention of a nation caught up in an industrial revolution. The dude ranches, and the allure of the fading West of the cowboy, opened that picture book up to this country and the rest of the world. It's hard to imagine another place on earth surpassing Jackson, WY, for its scenery. The Half Moon Ranch, situated on Cottonwood Creek in Moose, WY, just north of Jackson, with the regal Tetons for a backdrop, was as traditional a dude ranch as any. Founded in 1927, the Half Moon was among the earliest and more reputable of Jackson's many dude ranches. The ranch was incorporated in 1928 by the Karppi family and Anita Tarbell at a time when the dude ranches in and around Jackson really began to flourish.

A trio of brothers – the Eatons – is credited with opening the first dude ranch in the U.S., in 1882 in North Dakota. They later moved their operation to Wyoming near the Big Horn Range. The first Jackson dude ranch of record is the JY started by Struthers Burt and Louis Joy in 1908. Dude ranching, or dude wrangling if you prefer, built modern-day Jackson. Through the lure of early dude ranchers - providing among their primary activities horseback riding, pack trips, fishing, hunting, and an authentic western experience to mostly unfamiliar Easterners – the dude wranglers were responsible for igniting what was to become a hotbed of

Jackson tourism that has grown exponentially from the 1920s to the present. Those dude hosts easily were the most influential contributors, not just to the mountain West's vacation industry, but in writing Jackson's colorful history. Not only did dude ranches help paint an image of Jackson for outsiders, their attraction and notoriety were equally responsible for presenting and defining the modern day cowboy. The genuine article like Grant Beck

One had to go no further than the Half Moon to capture the essence of a Jackson dude ranch operation. The best description and definition of what dude wrangling was all about is portrayed in the following reprint of the Half Moon Ranch's 1930 brochure:

THE HALF MOON RANCH
FOR GIRLS
July 11 – August 30, 1930

The Half Moon Ranch for girls will open on July 11th for the season of 1930, under the direction of Miss Anita Tarbell and of Mr. and Mrs. Peter Karppi. The group will be limited to about fifteen girls, only those recommended by the staff or by personal friends being considered. Girls from the East will leave Boston and New York on July 8th, under the personal supervision of members of the staff. Others may join the party at any convenient point en route.

The group will travel by private car over the New York Central and Union Pacific Railroads to Rock Springs, Wyoming. From this point the journey will be completed by automobile over the desert to the scenic Hoback Canyon, through the frontier town of Jackson and across the sage brush flats to the Ranch.

The Half Moon Ranch is situated in the beautiful Jackson Hole country, at the foot of the snow-capped Teton Mountains on the border of the Teton National Park and about forty miles from the southern entrance to the Yellowstone Park. Five mountain lakes are within easy riding distance of the Ranch. All of the buildings are of the old-time western log construction. The main log cabin with living room and long porch and the dining room face the mountains and creek. Smaller cabins to accommodate two girls each are placed among the trees, within sound of rushing water. These cabins are attractively furnished with rustic furniture, rag rugs and gay cretonnes.

Life on the ranch has the simplicity of frontier days. The girls ride over the many game trails accompanied always by counselors and competent guides; they fish and swim in the creeks and mountain lakes, ride on the sage brush flats at dawn and dusk and frequently spend evening around the camp fire.

Pack Trips are made into the mountains to regions unknown to the average dude rancher. On these trips the girls ride over magnificent trails, across snow fields, and often through the fields of rare alpine flowers. They camp in pine forests, by lakes and mountain streams, sleep in tents or around the camp fire out under the stars. They fish for trout, swim in the lakes and they have the opportunity to see big game, moose, elk, deer, bear, and coyotes.

A group of campers at the Half Moon Ranch, 1952.

To complete the western experiences, the girls attend the famous Jackson rodeo, where they see the cowboys ride broncos, rope steers and race wild horses.

GENERAL INFORMATION

Each girl has a reliable western horse for the season, choosing her own horse if she prefers. It is not necessary for her to know how to ride as instruction is part of the fun.

The Ranch has an excellent doctor on staff and there is a well-equipped hospital in the immediate vicinity.

Simple, wholesome meals with plenty of fresh vegetables and fresh milk are provided under the direction of an experienced dietitian. Special attention has been given to all matters of sanitation, and the ranch has an ample supply of excellent drinking water.

The typical cowboy outfit of overalls, bright shirts and gay scarfs is recommended. These things may be purchased in the West. A list of personal equipment will be sent to all registered members of the party. Owing to the difficulty of transportation, all equipment should be packed in duffle bags or as hand luggage. All mail and parcel post packages should be addressed to the Half Moon Ranch, Moose Post Office, Jackson Hole, Wyoming. Telegrams should be sent to the same address via Victor, Idaho.

FEES

A charge of $650 will be made for the season. This amount will include all expenses at the ranch, a saddle horse for the season and the pack trips. Personal laundry is not included in this estimate. Transportation is additional and will be furnished at cost. There are but a few ways of spending money and each girl needs only a moderate allowance.

A registration fee of $150 must accompany each application. Registrations should be forwarded to the Directors at the earliest possible date. The remaining amount of $500 and transportation expenses are due on June 10th. All cheques should be made payable to the Half Moon ranch. No refund will be made in case of withdrawal from the party. Further information may be obtained from the Directors.

Grant Beck on his way to town in 1951.

Obviously, not all of Jackson's dude ranches limited their guests to girls. In later years the Half Moon, too, went co-ed. They attempted to provide their guests with a true western experience, albeit with comforts western ranch hands and cow punchers may have been unaccustomed to. The Half Moon was in operation from 1927 through 1962. Grant Beck hired on in 1950 and, at 25-years-of-age, was one of the valley's youngest ranch foremen. By then, Grant and his brother Wells, who had also spent a few summers at the Half Moon, had earned quite a reputation for being top hands. Grant was especially well-suited for dude wrangling. He was, and is, as comfortable around people of all ages, from all walks of life, as he is around horses of all breeds with any disposition. In his role at the ranch, Grant was as responsible for the campers as he was for the livestock. He has a lot of very fond memories of both.

"Do you know Lee Gilbert? He was my first dude boy - the first year I was at the Half Moon. We're still friends. He was the one I got my Dodge truck from. He really took to me. The Half Moon is where I got started. They went coed the first year I was there. We had six little boys and twelve girls. Worked there seven years. Fact the last summer I worked there is the

summer I bought the Two Bar Spear ranch. That was my first piece of land. To give you an idea on how land's a goin', I give $22,000 for those 320 acres in 1956. It had a house, a chicken coop and a barn on it; and the fence around the outside. That was it – that was all the improvements. The land was half-ass put into alfalfa, but they were goin' to try and get by. I surveyed it to see where the irrigation would go. It raised some hay, but didn't raise as much as I did the next year. But it still wasn't enough. And, by gosh, you couldn't irrigate it. So the second year, I started leveling ground. I leveled the whole damn thing, and I could do some good."

For the seven seasons that Grant was there the Half Moon was never short on young lads or lasses desiring to attend. The session was full every summer through word of mouth and referrals. This was a testament to both Miss Tarbell's initiative and the quality and skills of the staff she hired. But, according to Grant, there was an occasional albeit rare exception when it came to the perceived qualifications or presented abilities of a Half Moon counselor.

"Dexter Cheney – he was headmaster at Fountain Valley School in Colorado Springs. No common sense in anything he wanted to do. He got to the Half Moon with a saddle and new saddle blanket. 'Is it alright if I catch one of those horses and put my saddle on it, and get this saddle blanket to where it would fit?' he asked me.

Christ, if you're gonna ride it much at all, the sweat from the horse is enough to get it to break-in to where it will fit. I never did let a blanket soak like that. So he caught a horse, and he took that saddle blanket down the crick. Just threw it in and let it soak. He give $38 for it. Put it on this horse, and then his saddle. Cinched it up. About every 30 minutes he'd go tighten the cinch on his saddle agin. And the horse was tied to the hitchin' rack. I didn't say nothin'. Didn't ask what he was doin' or anything. You couldn't tell what color that blanket was when he took his saddle off. It was the only roan saddle blanket I ever saw!

.....And he decided the kids couldn't be clean enough by taking a bath every other day, or by swimmin' in the crick. Crick with fresh, clear water run right by the cabin. I think they oughta have hot water he said. He asked Ms. Tarbell if he could pick up a couple of barrels so they could have some hot water. They got some rocks, heated them in an open fire, and

placed them in one barrel. He'd have hot water in one barrel and cold in another. And a big tub they could put water in and wash their hair and stuff. So he could 'actually get those boys clean.' He went and brought a couple of tubs home, and barrels, you know. Got it all rigged up. Well this water, it was a really steamin'. You coulda scalded a hog it it! And one little boy washed his head in cold water. Got pretty clean I guess. He had soap in his eyes and went to rubbin' it out. Dexter said, 'Just a minute, I can rinse you off.' He got a bucket of that hot water and poured it on him – scalded that little boy. And that's when he and I split partnership. 'If you're a school teacher,' I said, 'you're one of the dumbest sons-of–a-bitch I ever run into. You call that common sense. You don't have any!'

I got that little boy and went down to Ms. Tarbell, down to her office. She got up and looked at him, and cried out, 'Oh, my! Grant would you take him into Doc McCloud? I think he's blistered pretty badly!' So I did. While I was gone they had quite a conversation about him and me. With the way I had talked to a school teacher. He wasn't the only teacher there was that I talked back to. I think he was towin' the mark from then on!"

Grant continued his memories of Dexter Cheney:

"Later that summer Dexter went up in the mountains on a pack trip with a - he wanted an all man crew. So, we hired Jules Farlow from Lander to cook. His brother Stub Farlow is the one they took the picture of on that buckin' horse and whose silhouette's on Wyoming license plates. Well, Jules is a good guy – a good cook. I don't know why Cheney wanted so damn many horses. He had 17 head of pack horses for about 16 people.

I went up there to help pack and I had a bronc horse – never shod. I'd just had him broke to lead. So I hog-tied him and threw him down. Tied his two left legs together and the two right ones, stuck a pole in between 'em, off over his rump, where I could hold his feet up. I shod him in about an hour. Once in a while I had two little boys come over and sit on that poke to hold it steady. I was shoein' that colt while Cheney was packin' up.

Why pretty soon Cheney, he'd tied panniers on a really good saddle horse instead of one of the pack horses we'd had. Ol' Frosty, the saddle horse he'd packed, was our head counselor's horse. She'd rode that horse at camp the past nine years – 16-hands and a helluva good travelin' horse – but had never carried a pack in its life. The school teacher was goin' to pack what he thought needed packed. Cheney thought he knew more about it than I did. I just said, 'Let that son-of-a-bitch go ahead.' I was busy shoein' this bronc.

Pretty soon ol' Frosty blew-up and dumped everything that Cheney'd put on his back. Dexter says,

'You mean to tell me somebody rides this horse?'

'Yeah, they have for nine years, Miss Tarbell tells me.'

'He must've been quite a cowboy!'

'Well I guess she was a pretty good rider,' Grant replied sarcastically.

Dexter Cheney had no idea of who did what with any of the horses. He may have known the difference between a pack horse and riding horse but didn't bother asking Grant or anyone else at the Half Moon for any direction or input. Some horses are trained to be both packed and ridden. But a horse that has never been packed usually reacts pretty adversely the first time. Frosty was one of the better riding horses on the ranch. For the most part the horse had annually been ridden by one of the lady camp counselors. Grant found it quite amusing that Cheney assumed that Frosty was too spirited to be ridden by anyone except the best or most accomplished horseman.

"He had nothin' more to say. After I got done shoein', why, I rode ol' Frosty around a little bit and said,

'Why don't you put one of them bigger boys on him – he'll be fine.'

'Looks like he handles pretty good.'

'Yep.'

'I think I'll ride him,' Cheney says.

'As long as you treat him like he's a horse, you'll probably be alright!'"

Back to the headmaster's first pack trip:

"Cheney led the group to the Half Moon's high-country camp. There were actually two camp sites. One camp was at a little higher elevation than the other. By the time they'd moved to the second, the higher camp, the temperature had dropped significantly and it'd snowed. I don't know where the hell Cheney's head was – probably in his hind end. Anybody with a little common sense would've turned them horses and kids around and headed back down to the ranch.

Cheney'd been leadin' two pack horses: the one carryin' the eggs, silverware, and cook stove; and another one carryin' other supplies but no food. I guess he just thought the other pack horses would follow 'em. I don't know why but they should've been all tied together with lead lines and led as one long pack string. So when they got to the second camp, they had only six pack horses of the 17 they'd started out with. None of the pack horses with food packed on 'em except eggs. The eggs was all broken cuz they hadn't been packed right. The camp cook, Jules Farlow, he'd seen that those kids was hungry as he was. So Jules, the only adult with any sense, hiked up to the highway - up by Togwotee Pass. He walked out of the wilderness area up there and caught a ride down to the ranch. I was still down at the ranch still shoein' horses. Pretty soon here Jules comes walkin' up to me.

'What happened now?'

He says, 'Ms. Tarbell here?'

'I think so.'

'Well, I'm quittin'!'

'Well,' I said, 'you'll have to tell that to her yourself. I'm just a horseshoer.'

So Jules, he went to turn in his notice to Ms. Tarbell and tell her what'd happened. Scared Ms. Tarbell to death. She'd never had anything like that happen at the Half Moon in the 25 years or so since it started. She'd come out and told me what the problem was and I'd asked her if she had had any hotdogs in storage. She'd said,

'No.'

'Ain't no need to go out half-cocked. Why don't you go in and call Harriet, Hickey we called her. See if she could drive out from Jackson and bring some food. I'll pack it in and my bedroll.'"

Half Moon Ranch corrals about 1952 after Grant Beck had rebuilt them.

Harriet "Hickey" Johnston had been a Half Moon counselor off and on for several years and was living in town – Jackson – at the time.

In actuality, Grant was the Half Moon foreman. He was a little bent based on Dexter Cheney having been hired on and assigned the responsibility of the kids and the pack trip. It infuriated Grant even more that, in his mind, Cheney didn't know the first thing about horsemanship. Grant was always the go-to person at the ranch if there was anything wrong with anything. Everyone – Ms. Tarbell, the staff, and the kids – had always come to Grant if they needed anything done or just needed some advice. Cheney had pretty much showed up one day and assumed control. Grant vented his frustration on Jules Farlow.

"I knew damn well there was a problem. Jules wasn't even sure where they'd camped. I figured if there's snow up there it would be on Togowotee Pass. So that's where I headed. I'd left the ranch at about 10:30 the next morning, trailered up and unloaded the horses on top of

the Pass. It'd taken me about two hours to get to the trailhead where I entered the wilderness area with the horses. I rode about 16 miles downhill towards where I figured Cheney and the kids would be. I found 'em. I'd led one pack horse in with me. When I come up to the camp, the kids was sittin' around a big camp fire, half-dressed, and cold. If they weren't happy to see somebody! They were pretty hungry. At least they'd had a pretty good fire a goin'. I told two or three of the older boys to go cut some willows – if you could find 'em – or sticks to roast marshmallows. I'd packed marshmallows and four big packages of hotdogs. From one Jules'd said, they had the pack horse carryin' the camp stove in camp. The hot dog buns should've been packed in the stove with the eggs. After they rounded up the sticks, I handed the hot dogs to Dexter and got ready to pull-out of camp to ride out and find the missin' pack horses. Dexter says to me,

'You want help in findin' those horses?'

'No, I'll find 'em.'

I knew the trail from where they were camped and headed down. I'd told the wrangler, Jim, why you'd better gather some firewood, I don't know how long this storm is going to last. He was grouchy, cold, and hungry as those kids. About 5:30 I come back into camp with the pack horses. I'd found 'em all together. Not a one had rolled or slipped a pack. They'd been gone two nights and a day, and were about five to six miles from camp. They was sure wantin' them packs off!

So I got 'em all in pretty good shape. The snow had stopped and started to melt a little. The pack horses got a drink and some grass. I told them to just stay here in this big meadow until somebody comes back to get 'em outta this mess.

Cheney didn't come back a second year. He was under me as far as reportin' to somebody at the ranch, but he didn't want it that way. It bugged him a lot because he was all educated and I was just a cowboy."

Grant's last season at the Half Moon ended in the fall of 1956. With the wealth of experiences and knowledge garnered from his years working for Ms. Tarbell, Grant, and his first wife Ellie, started their own summer camp and dude ranch - the Two Bar Spear Ranch - located just outside of Pinedale, WY. The scenery in which the town of Pinedale sets is not nearly as picturesque as the Jackson valley. But the Jim Bridger Wilderness and Wind River Mountain Range, with trailheads accessible minutes from Pinedale, offer every bit as breathtaking panorama and pack trip setting as any I know of.

Grant Beck, and his third wife – Abie, still operate a girls-only summer camp at the Two Bar Spear. In fact, you could pretty much replace the date on the Half Moon Ranch brochure from 1930 to today, and you'd experience the same wonderful attributes and benefits. Each year at the Two Bar Spear's girls' camp, much like the tradition of the Half Moon Ranch of yesteryear, there are never any openings. The Becks haven't needed to advertise for campers in some 46 years. This can be attributed to the warmth, hospitality, and care Grant and Abie shower on each camper and every guest.

Grant and Abie Beck at Section Corner Lake in the Wind River Mountain Range in 1997.

Pick-up Man

Jackson Rodeo.

Chapter Eleven

I'M A LOVER, NOT A FIGHTER

Cowboys are tough. If you don't believe me, go watch a rodeo. Better yet, volunteer to spend a weekend rounding up, tossing, and branding calves. Or, spend ten hours on horseback riding mountain trails – for 30 straight days. My second go-around in my first and last saddle bronc event was further evidence to convince me. It was 1978 in the Kansas City Rodeo at Benjamin Ranch. The Sankey family, out of Rosehill, KS, was the rough stock contractor. I'd drawn a horse listed in the program as Pitchfork. My memory's pretty foggy after coming out of the chute. I spurred the horse when the gate swung open and, true to its name, the horse pitched me right over his head – long before the eight-second count. What seemed like an eternity went by when I finally collected myself enough to find my way out of the arena. To this day I don't remember how I got home. When the dust cleared from the blow to my noggin, I distinctly remember Sally, my wife, giving me an ultimatum: "Me or the rodeo." I loved her then, and we're still married. That was my last time on a rodeo buckin' horse.

I still help Grant brand his calves in the spring each year. After a full day of throwing calves you know you've done somethin'. It's hard to imagine doing it everyday. But there are cowboys who do. They're tough. The toughest cowboys are most generally the ones who don't brag about how tough they are. Being sturdy is just part of the cowboy way. Grant Beck's about as tough a person as I've ever known.

I knew Grant was tough when I first met him in 1976. Sure, part of that was his coarse-looking exterior: skin weathered like well-used leather chaps that's gone way too long without oil or conditioner; a toughness that's reflected in his eyes and in his spirit. It's a part of him. A sturdiness resulting from the hard life he's chosen but never complained about. To a kid who'd pretty much grown up in the city, Grant was intimidating. At 19, I was pretty fearless. I outweighed Grant by at least 40 pounds and was about three inches shorter. But at 5' 11", 175 pounds, I wouldn't have been referred to as being strapping. Grant was someone I knew I never wanted to tussle with. Most people who knew Grant through the years felt the same way. There was no quit in Grant. He never backed down from anything or anyone, particularly when he was in the right.

Grant never looked for a brawl. He wasn't shy either. I think it was his western-spirited confidence more than anything that kept him out of what could have been a great many confrontations.

In the 1950s Grant was a pick-up man in the weekly Jackson, WY, rodeos. In bareback riding and saddle bronc riding events, the pick-up men kept the contestants safe helping them off their mounts after the eight-second bell sounded. Literally "picking them up" right off the horse they had drawn to ride. For a ride to be legal, and scored by the judges, both hands must remain free of the rigging and saddle until eight seconds are up.

"I'm amazed about how few fights I had in my life. As old as I am you know damn well there were fights. I never did have a fight in Jackson Hole. Yeah, I did too!

A guy I picked-up at the rodeo. He was belly-achin' cuz he'd thought he'd had an eight-second ride. He was a bareback rider. Everybody thought he was pretty tough. Red Ramsey was his name from Lander, WY. Nobody ever questioned him at all. I was right beside'em, ready to pick'em up. The bell rang. Before the bell rang he'd had a hold of that bareback riggin' – both hands – and I went in to grab him - I waited until the bell.

About as close to me and you I picked him up. They "no scored him" when the judges seen both his hands on the bareback riggin' before the eight-second bell. He was arguin' with the judge. I said, 'that is correct.' I had him, ready to pull him off. Both his hands were on the riggin' before the bell. Gosh it was close to the judges' stand.

After the rodeo there was always a dance in all the bars in Jackson. The rodeo would be over by a quarter to ten each Saturday evenin'. Everybody'd go to town. I had my pick-up horse turned loose. Eleanor, my first wife, and I was goin' together. So that night we went in to town, to the Log Cabin Bar. Red come over and started tellin' me how tough he was. Purdy soon, his language got pretty bad. I said, 'Well, we might as well just go out in the street cuz I think you're too dumb to know how to talk. I don't think you can fight any better.' We went out. He had a lot longer reach than I had and was about 30 pounds heavier. Once we got outside he took a wild swing at me. I hit'em under his arm and never laid off poundin' his guts. I ruptured his spleen. They went out there to see why he wouldn't get up. They took him to the hospital. It was the only fight I ever had in Jackson Hole.

As much as I went to Jackson, played and danced, that was my only fight. I had a helluva good time up there all my life."

Grant Beck aboard Yeller.

Grant's still tough. I can only hope that when I'm 70-something years old that I can still climb aboard a horse and spend all day roping and dragging calves to the fire to brand. Grant's resiliency never ceases to amaze me.

Clure Smith, a round-up foreman, on the left and Wells Beck on the right. A little clowning for the camera, about 1944.

Chapter Twelve

COWBOYS

JUST GOTTA HAVE FUN

All his life, Grant Beck's been a cowboy. And all of his life he's had fun. I have never known anyone who's been so content with his chosen lot in life. In fact, Grant, to my knowledge, has never even uttered the word regret. When I get caught up in the fast- paced, multi-task-demanding world in which we live, I visit Grant to get grounded. Whether going to his Pinedale, WY, ranch or his Florence, MO, cattle farm, the surroundings are not what make the difference. It's sitting down with a cup of "camp" coffee and visiting. He doesn't even have to be spinning his yarns. And there is nothing more relaxing or mind-cleansing than spending a day or two on horseback.

Grant is both smart and clever. Not school-book smart, but the sort of intelligence stemming from the sense of always knowing what's going on around you. Don't let the fact that he dropped out of school at 13 fool you. Grant embodies the adage, "dumb like a fox." His most endearing quality is his sense of humor. An important ingredient in having a good sense of humor is the ability to laugh at yourself – find humor in one's own mistakes. That seems to ease the guilt of laughing at someone else. Grant takes it a step further – practical joker. It's not that Grant can't be serious, he can actually be intimidating. Those who have worked for him know this well. Grant always manages to find the lighter side of things. He keeps everyone around him cheerful if not just a little off-balanced.

Grant's jokes at others' expense aren't usually cruel. But if someone really deserves it – watch out!

> *"I never had anybody up there at the Half Moon Ranch I could send down the trail. That time I hired, actually Ms. Tarbell hired, Dexter Cheney, a headmaster from the Fountain Valley School in Colorado Springs. It was a private boarding school. Thank God it weren't me who hired him. Cheney was about 40. He brought a kid along with him that was supposed to be his helper. Jim was about 16-years-old and was six-foot-two. Not as heavy as you are. Damn, me*

and Johnny, we really got a kick out of him. Jim really tried to show what a cowboy he was. Hell, he had no more common sense than that headmaster did.

We didn't know a damn thing about Jim, me and Johnny. Johnny Johnson had the cabinet shop up in Jackson – just before you got into Jackson. He's sold that now and is still alive. Me and Johnny'd got to visitin' about Jim, back then at the Half Moon, and what horses to save for him to ride. We had a horse there we hadn't tried yet. Ms. Tarbell said that it had just quit buckin' out at the Jackson Rodeo. It had a #2 branded on its hip. It was a bally-faced, buckskin, stockin'-legged mare. They'd called her Cream Puff at the rodeo grounds. That's what old Walt Callahan who owned the rodeo had told me. So that's what we called her. Johnny and I had rode all the ranch horses except that one. Saved her for Jim. Me and Johnny never took time to pick up the cobble stones in the corral. The corral was on this rocky hill. There were two or three horses that could actually buck a little. We figured this one definitely could, comin' from the rodeo an' all.

Horse-breaking corral at the Half Moon Ranch – Grant's turn.

Each mornin', Johnny and I flipped a coin to see who got first pick of horses to ride that day after we'd got 'em all gathered. It seemed, no matter who won, every damn one I picked had some buck in him. We had this horse called Ike that Johnny drawed one mornin'. So he got him in the corral and everything was fine, goin' good. Johnny says let's ride down to Moose Junction. We had to ride past the Church of the Transfiguration – that's where we'd drive the car or ride our horses to church. We could drive across the bridge, tie-up, and get a drink at the bar near there without anybody knowin' it. Anyway, we took off toward Moose, Johnny on Ike and me on the last one I'd saddled. Before we got to the bridge, why Johnny and Ike had the best rodeo we'd had all summer. We kept Ike all summer. That was the only horse that give us any trouble.

Jim was really anxious to demonstrate his cowboy skills. Johnny and me got Cream Puff into the corral one mornin'. Jim got all ready to ride so he picked up all the rocks and tossed them outta the corral before he'd even caught her. Jim was throwin' all these rocks out of the corral. Didn't have the sense to throw 'em slowly. The horse didn't know whether he was throwin' 'em at her or not. So he had her riled up a little by doin' that. Johnny just about let the cat-out-of-the-bag about Cream Puff bein' a bucking horse from the rodeo.

'Damn that's a pretty brand on her hip.' Jim said.

'Hell,' I said, 'It's just a printed two ain't it?'

'Yeah, pretty neat.'

Jim didn't pick up on it that the branded "2" was her number in the rodeo string. Didn't know any better. Pretty quick he got the rocks gathered-up, went and caught the horse. Had a hell of a time catchin' her. He finally got her caught. Tied her up. He turned her head this away and that away with her bridle and reins, you know. He started to get on her. He teetered in the stirrup for awhile. Pulled his foot outta the stirrup and turned her around. Give her plenty of time to think of what to do if he was to get on her back. If you get on one right away, they don't have time to figure it out. Cream Puff figured that Jim wasn't goin' to hurt her and she calmed down. Jim got on, threw his leg over her back, and yelled whoa. I looked at Johnny and said,

'Let's go to the bunkhouse.'

'You guys goin' up to the bunkhouse?' Jim said nervously.

'Yeah, hell, we waited here 15 minutes,' I said.

'Well, I think I'll be alright,' with not much self-assurance.

'Well, if you're not, holler at us.'

After all of our plannin' and connivin', me and Johnny's, and all the time Jim spent tryin' to avoid an accident, Cream Puff never even bucked – never did anything stupid. I actually think that mare had a nice walk.

We had more fun with Jim all summer. We picked out another horse for Jim to ride. One that all it wanted to do was a jig. There was this little black horse that me and Johnny kidded about what a good horse he was. Wasn't worth a gosh damn. Jim wanted to know if he could ride him. We said sure. We had more fun watchin' him try to figure out what to do on a horse that didn't know nothin'. Jim didn't know a good one from a bad one. But he sure thought he was a cowboy. Hell, the dude kids that come up to camp that summer knew more about how to ride a horse than he did – and some of them had never ridden.

Jim stopped by the Two Bar Spear Ranch here a while back. He grew up to be alright. I kinda felt bad about all the trouble we give'm He's still 6'4", but weighs over 200 lbs. now – he really filled out. I don't think he ever thought we was bein' mean to him. It wasn't anything more than some good o'l fun. I think he kinda appreciated the time Johnny and me spent with him trying to teach him somethin' about horses. I sure was surprised to see him. Made me fill good that he made the effort and all."

Funny thing about Grant Beck, through all the years, even the horses and people that he doesn't take to, seem to take to him.

Grant Beck grooming a three-year-old mare he owned at the Half Moon Ranch. He broke and trained this mare for a 14-year-old dude girl – Annie Gamble, of the Procter & Gamble lineage.

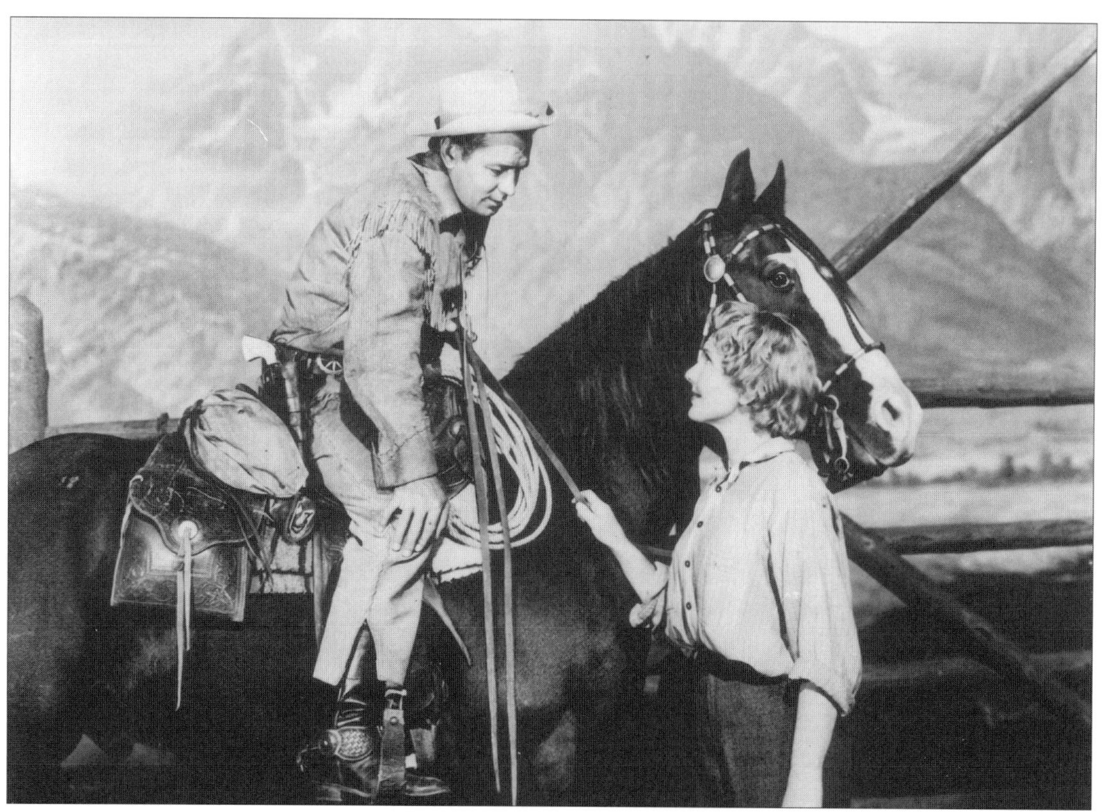

Alan Ladd and Jean Arthur in a scene from *Shane*.

Chapter Thirteen

YOU'RE PRETTY CAPABLE

"You're pretty capable," quipped Alan Ladd to Grant Beck.

If Academy Awards were presented to the most beautiful natural settings, *Shane* would have been nominated for seven. What could provide a more majestic background than the Grand Tetons outside Jackson Hole? The vistas around Jackson provide as much an ageless beauty as *Shane* is a timeless western classic. Justification for this wondrous backdrop was somewhat realized in the film's sole Oscar out of six nominations. The golden statue was carried away by A. B. Guthrie, Jr., for Best Color Cinematography. Actor Alan Ladd's comments during filming were as good as another award for one of the film's extras – Grant Beck. Grant had taken a two-week leave of absence from his job at the Half Moon Ranch on the chance of earning some of that Hollywood per diem. Ranch hands of that era took kindly to any opportunity to bring home a little extra cash.

The year was 1953. The sleepy town of Jackson still had some dirt streets. The unseasonably dry summer created problems for one of the scenes they were filming. The script called for wagons ambling along a dirt road as they might have decades earlier. Hence, they needed wagon ruts. Although it was not uncommon for replica wagons to be seen hauling dude kids around in those days, the majority of traffic in and around Jackson was in the form of horseless carriages – most locals called those pick-up trucks. The dirt roads were more hard-packed than usual from the lack of rain. In true Hollywood style, the film's crew would be appropriately creative – in this case making ruts. With a team of horses and a plow, in short order they'd produce a set of wagon ruts. As often the case, this turned out much easier said than done. Especially for some of the Hollywood crew who may have been just a little on the greenhorn side.

In Grant's words:

"It was dryer than hell! The crew had a hell of a time with this team of horses. They had

em-a-goin this away and the plow jumpin' plum out of the ground. Couldn't get that team slowed enough to get the plow started. I went out there in this silly costume, stove-pipe pants with a dude hat, and that guy was tickled to death to give somebody else that team. He couldn't do nothin' with them. He was supposed to be a stagehand or somethin'. I took hold of the team. I stood on the doubletree so I had something to brace to, so I could hold 'em down. I asked a guy standin' behind me,

'Hold them handles so I can plow them furrows.'

They had a water truck. So they drove the water truck along side of me fillin' the furrows full of water as I was plowin the one next to it - for the other rut. It worked out good. I got the plowin' done. This guy come out to me after all that, the one I took the plow handles from, and he took my picture. I should've asked for one but I didn't."

Grant has several fond memories from that shoot. Of course he had no idea what the outcome of the movie might be, or the acclaim *Shane* would still be getting 50 years later. He does remember visiting with Brandon de Wilde, the boy Joey in the movie, and watching him get in what mischief he could when off camera. He also remembers filming being halted one day and everybody gathering around a birthday cake to sing happy birthday to Alan Ladd's daughter, Alana. As memorable as it all was, it wouldn't be Grant's last brush with Hollywood.

Grant remarking on Alan Ladd:

"He was a real friendly, decent person; a kind, prince of a person."

Set from the movie *Shane*.

Chapter Fourteen

THE TWO BAR SPEAR RANCH BRAND

Branding livestock dates back to 2700 B.C. Of course, in Egypt brands took the form of hieroglyphics. In some ancient cultures it wasn't just the livestock that had a mark burned into their flesh; it was also common practice with slaves. Hernando Cortez is credited in bringing branding to the Americas from Spain in 1541. There has never been a better or more permanent way to claim or prove ownership of one's livestock than a hot iron.

Brands are issued and registered through state-run agencies. They can expire. And just because you have the brand registered in one state does not automatically provide you with the right to claim it in another. If one's desire was to ranch, with the intent of raising cattle or horses, it was highly recommended to secure a brand and get it registered. Still today, the brand inspector's office in a person's home state can help with the selection. They'll determine if a brand desired is available.

The history of brands in the U.S. is fascinating. Each brand has a story. Many brand owners can recite their brand's history. Some of the more colorful stories have to do with how a cowboy or ranch acquired their brand. Grant got hold of the Two Bar Spear brand in about as unorthodox a fashion as any, I suspect.

> *"I got that brand in '53 - in July, the first part of July - the 4th. The guy I got it from was Pete Peters. He had this Two Bar Spear brand. I was with him one night in the Log Cabin Saloon in Jackson. I'd known him from the year before. My first wife Eleanor was with me. It was right after we come back. We'd took a week off. We'd come over from Pinedale back to Jackson. I quit the Half Moon Ranch that year and run that J Bar S outfit. You know the Circle S? The next ranch above it. That's where we spent our first year, Eleanor and I.*
>
> *Pete'd had the brand but it wasn't on another animal. He'd just wrote up and sent to the*

state brand inspection office to see if he could get it, and got it. Part of that was Eleanor and I had wrote up and sent in for four or five brands to Cheyenne. Christ, the only one they offered us of any we sent in were all for the left side. Pete got the Two Bar Spear brand for the right side. That was a lot better than the left side - a lot handier to put on.

I had a pair of boots on. They had crepe soles. I was ridin' a wide stirrup on my saddle. Damn, them boots felt good! Just felt like sponge under your feet you know? Ya wouldn't hardly feel your weight. Pete didn't know it. The only thing I said to pump him up was that they were the most comfortable boots I ever had. I said, 'Whadda ya take for that brand?'

'I'll trade it to you for that pair of boots.'

'Write out a bill of sale'

So I pulled my boots off and give 'em to him, right there at the bar. He wrote out a bill of sale. The bartender witnessed it. It read: Pete Peters trades the Two Bar Spear brand out to Grant Beck for a pair of cowboy boots. It was 'bout a half a block from the Log Cabin Bar to this dry goods store where I bought 'em. I went down there and bought another pair of the exact same boots for $35. Gosh they were good!"

Now, the Two Bar Spear brand is registered in three states: Wyoming, Idaho, and Missouri. It's registered in Grant's name along with Abigail Beck's, his third and current wife.

Grant Beck just finishing branding a 3-year-old Appaloosa colt at Dr. Boyce's place, sometime between 1963 and 1964.

Banty Bowlsby in his later years.

Chapter Fifteen

BANTY BOWLSBY

With a name like Banty there is bound to be a good story or two. Arthur William "Banty" Bowlsby was born on June 13, 1897, in Hay Springs, NE. According to the Jackson Hole Historical Society and Museum, he earned his nickname because he was "small and always on the fight." His family moved from Nebraska to Wyoming at the turn of the century. Banty's dad Bill homesteaded a parcel of land in the Basin around 1900. The original homestead is now part of the Campbell Ranch in Bondurant. There are undoubtedly enough stories pertaining to Banty's life to fill another book. After all, in his 96 years of living in and around the Bondurant area, he is credited with a great many things – not all true – not the least of which he was rumored to have had seven different wives.

Grant's recollections of Banty are primarily concerned with Banty's prowess as an elk hunter. According to Grant,

> *"Banty was the best elk hunter Jackson has ever seen. And the best shot too!"*

According to Grant, Banty had one very distinguishable feature:

> *"You could tell Banty anywhere because there was a piece missin' out of his ear. When he was young, his family couldn't afford central heating. Banty slept under his blankets with a couple of their dogs every night to keep warm. One night the dogs got to wrestlin' while under Banty's covers. Somehow he got between 'em when a full blown dogfight erupted. In the middle of the fracus, one of the dogs nipped a piece outta one of his ears."*

Banty was a long-time Wyoming outfitter. After he'd established his reputation as Jackson's premier elk hunter, there was a period of time in the mid to late '50s, when Banty got many of his referrals for hunters through the Wort Hotel in Jackson. Some of you may have heard of, or been to, the world-famous Silver Dollar Bar in The Wort Hotel – one of Jackson's oldest. I believe it is there where I had my first beer in Jackson over 25 years ago.

For those of you unfamiliar with The Wort Hotel, it's been a Jackson Hole landmark since its opening in 1941. Charles Wort, the hotel's founder, homesteaded in South Park country, just outside of Jackson Hole, in 1893. In 1915, he bought four lots in what was later to be part of downtown Jackson, just a couple of blocks from present-day Jackson Square. The "luxury hotel," built at what was believed to be a cost of $90,000, opened in 1941 on those same four lots – those lots having spent the prior seven years as a horse corral and livery stable. The Silver Dollar Bar was added to the hotel in 1950 and so-named as the German cabinetmaker that designed and built the bar inlaid the top of it with 2,032 uncirculated silver dollars that had been obtained from the Denver Mint. The hotel burned to the ground in 1980, but was rebuilt and re-opened in 1981. The Wort is a popular tourist destination and is considered as one of the "Great Hotels of the West." You can stay there for the night or just stop by for a cold beer.

Banty Bowlsby starting the next generation early.

Grant's first job guiding hunters and packing out game was with Banty in 1955. Banty was an individual one could learn a lot from. He'd cut his teeth the hard way. Although he chose a relatively simple existence, there was nothing easy about life in Wyoming in his day. As a hunter, he was reputed simply as being one of the best. Although today some of his practices in hunting camp, with his hunters and the game they pursued, would be construed as less than ethical, he never harvested an elk or deer that someone had not purchased a tag for. There was always the question of who'd actually shot it. A practice of shooting game for someone who is less than skillful with a firearm is technically illegal by Wyoming Fish and Game standards, and is neither permitted nor tolerated. Fifty years ago it was likely a bit more challenging to enforce. Prior to signing on with Banty, Grant had heard plenty.

"Banty was known in the outfitter world as one of those who 'guaranteed meat.' After working for him I knew why. He always had a couple extree elk hangin' in a tree somewhere for his less fortunate, less skillful hunters."

Grant continued reminiscing about his first hunting season:

"Banty's killed more elk in Wyoming than anyone. I believe I packed out 85 elk that season. Banty could smell elk. We were sittin' by the campfire and Banty was fryin' up some bacon early one morning. He handed me the skillet. 'Keep an eye on this,' Banty said. We had four hunters in camp. All of a sudden, Banty, in a sudden flurry, rounded 'em up and headed up the hill. Purdy soon I heard gunfire, and looked up the hill. A herd of elk'd come over the ridge above camp. Guns were blazin'. All I could see were elk a fallin'. When the firin' had stopped a total of nine elk were down. Temporarily distracted, it come to what I was suppose' to be doin' – cookin' the bacon. When I looked down at the skillet, there weren't none left. The bacon'd all burnt up."

Generally when Grant starts his story telling, one story leads right into another. Reminiscing about Banty, this time was no different,

"I'd been packin' out elk all day and was worn to the bone. I got back to camp about 9 p.m. Banty would have done well to feed both his help and his horses a little better. That whole season I lived off Hershey bars – the big ones. Well, when I got back to camp, Banty said,

'I need ya to do some wranglin' for me a little later.'

I put up my horse, which was more overworked than me. Banty would have to find me a fresh mount 'bout every week. My older brother Wells would bring me a fresh horse – supposedly broke, which can't have been ridden more than a couple of times. He'd trade me for the one I had pretty much just broke for him. About 2:30 a.m. Banty woke me up and asked me to go wrangle some horses. Well, I was ridin' in the pitch dark when all of a sudden my mount stepped then lunged into a pond. Now I was wet and tired! I stayed on the horse as he lunged clear to the end of the pond. When he come out, it was right where the missin' horses that I was suppose' to be wranglin' were standin'. My horse, he must've smelled 'em. I got back to camp with the horses and all Banty wanted to know, with me lookin' at him like a drowned, starvin'rat, was what had taken me so long,

'And, by the way, how come yer all wet?'"

Having guided and wrangled for Grant in hunting camp, I can attest to the reality that there is always a lot to do and never enough time or help to do it. A typical day in hunting camp started at 4:00 a.m. The cook stove would get fired up – the camp coffee on. Breakfast fixins were gathered; fresh water fetched. Horses and pack mules were wrangled and fed. By 5:30 a.m. it was time to roust the hunters. Hopefully a plan had been devised in the prior hour and a half for the day's hunt. While the hunters ate their breakfast, horses were saddled and lunches made. If everything came off without a hitch, all were in the saddle and ready to go with plenty of time to spare before sun-up. The easy part was done.

No two days hunting were ever the same. A lot depended on what game was being hunted and where they were last seen, how many hunters were there, and, of course, the weather. Those were the normal variables. Then you had everything else imaginable that might interfere or adjust the best-laid plans and intentions. Of course you never knew where you might come across the game that matched the permit and, if a hunter was successful, where one might be when you needed to gut the animal and pack it out. You could always count on it not being easy. The pack animals needed to cart the game out were typically left at the most inconvenient place – like back at the packing corral. Whoever was wrangling horses would need to ride back to camp, anywhere from an hour to a half-a-day away, retrieve the pack mules, and begin the arduous process which was culminated when the harvested game was suspended from a tree near camp. Of course, during this time it was most generally the goal to get the hunters back to camp before dark. That didn't happen with any regularity. All that needed to be done then was make sure any fresh game was taken care of properly, unsaddle and brush the horses and mules, feed and water them, make sure the saddles, bridles, and blankets were stored properly, fetch fresh water, get the camp coffee boiling as quickly as possible, make sure that any and all of the hunters' special needs were being met, get dinner cooking, inventory the food for both the hunters and the livestock, double-checking quantities, feed the hunters, be jovial and tell stories, check the horses and mules, fetch water to boil and do dishes, and hopefully, get the hunters to bed down at a reasonable hour. You can imagine how things might be complicated during a rain or snow storm. If everything went somewhat to plan, midnight would be a plausible time to hit your bedroll – which, hopefully, was dry. And, you guessed it, start all over again at 4:00 a.m!

Grant recalled one of those irregular variables from that first hunting season with Banty:

"I was responsible for keepin' track of the groceries. One time I found a couple pounds of ground beef missin'. I figured I'd fool the ol' girl – sow black bear. The next day while the hunters went fishin', I hid in the cook tent. Sure enough 'bout mid-morning the black bear came saunterin' into camp. Come right into the mess tent. When I seen her front paws and muzzle, I jumped out my hidin' spot and hollered at her. She casually scampered away. Well, I decided to sleep in the cook tent that night. When I woke up the next mornin', she'd snuck back in the tent while I was sleepin' and made off with two more pounds of ground beef.

Other than that, we never really had much problems with bears though."

Grant Beck said he'd know Banty Bowlsby's pack string anywhere because Banty was one of the few outfitters who used a squaw hitch on his packs.

Mark Pearson leading Two Bar Spear Ranch horses through Pinedale, ca. 1980.

Chapter Sixteen

A BAD WRECK

Pinedale, WY, was, and is, no different than a lot of towns out West when it comes to livestock. By the light of day, horses and cattle own the roads. In other words, legally, they have the right-of-way while the sun is still up. Behind the wheel of a car, one just always needs to be on the defensive. I fully grasped the meaning of this in the early spring of 1976.

John Roup – an Indiana transplant to Boulder, WY – had been negotiating with a local horse trader. He was trying to work out a deal on leasing a few head of riding and packing horses for the summer fishing and pack season. There were about 20 head of mostly unbroke horses the trader needed to move from Boulder to a pasture just on the south edge of Pinedale, about ten miles up the road. The route was along Route 191, a two-lane highway that runs from Rock Springs through Boulder and Pinedale, up to Jackson. Since I owned a horse – albeit just barely broke – and some free time, I was recruited to help drive this small herd. Although not much of a horse expert at the time, it didn't take an expert to realize that this bunch was a bit on the skittish side, thereby providing a real challenge.

My biggest concern was in keeping them moving along the highway as close to the fence and as far away from pavement and on-coming traffic as possible. There were two riders and one truck trailing up the highway behind us as a blocker. Bud, who I'd renamed Sundance in deference to Robert Redford's character opposite Paul Newman as Butch Cassidy, was a three-year-old green-broke gelding. I'd purchased him from Grant Beck that May. He may have been from good stock, but at this point didn't know anymore about the appropriate conduct for this task than I. Both the horse and I knew more what to do than Roup and his mount.

Somehow we got within about two miles of our final destination with nary an incident, when all of a sudden, just as we were feeling like we'd accomplished something, a big black gelding, about 1,200 pounds, darted left out of the horse pack smack in front of an oncoming Jeep. The sound on impact which followed was not pleasant. The horse fell dead in his tracks – killed on impact. The front of the Jeep crumpled clear to the windshield. Somehow the lady driving was physically unscathed but emotionally, well, she was pretty shook-up. There wasn't much we could do except try to keep the rest of the horses corralled quietly along the fence, away from their dead companion, and wait for the sheriff. After what seemed liked an eternity, word had been relayed to the sheriff's department and a patrolman showed up on the scene. Much to my surprise, the poor gal staring at her totaled vehicle – the front-end propped up on a dead horse – was handed a ticket.

Believe me when I tell you there is absolutely nothing she could have done to avoid the accident. I felt more responsible than anyone else. When I thought about how much the horse trader was going to get from her in reimbursing him the value of his horse, I knew exactly what the livestock right of way business was all about. Later, when Grant told me about one of his "wrecks," I had better understanding and appreciation of the emotion. Only in Grant's accident, the driver was clearly at fault. Every year, twice a year – spring and fall – Grant trailed the Half Moon Ranch horse herd from Moose, WY, to Lorenzo, ID. It was about 140 miles - one way! The horses were led and driven right over Teton Pass and across the Snake River to and from a pasture that was leased every winter. The trip generally took two days – if there weren't any unforeseen happenings.

Grant Beck driving cattle to new pasture.

"I had one hell of a wreck – lost four head of horses and another 13 or so hurt. I was in the city limits with the herd. It was potato plantin' time. This farmer's son – he never had any brakes on his truck – had a truckload of seed potatoes on a two-ton truck. He come in through this herd of horses – in the city limits – about 25 or 40 miles per hour. Christ, talk about a wreck! I was ridin' with these horses, a tryin' to hold 'em down, so I could get 'em to the stock-yards. It was 'bout a half mile ahead of me. And this dumbass, when he hit the first horse, he panicked, and must've floored it. Had a little boy with him, four or five years old. I was ridin' a pretty good horse, who could handle about anything. Good thing he was, cuz I was tryin' to get these horses outta the way when he sped up. I had to shoot four head right on the spot.

Had 13 more that were all banged up.

So I went in, when I got to the pen in Newdale, ID – the railroad pen, about 70 miles from Jackson where I'd started from. I got everything in the pen. There was about this much daylight – it was dusk. Eleanor, my first wife, and Roy Ransom was helpin' me trail. Roy was a bartender at the Log Cabin Saloon in Jackson. He was also a good hand when someone needed help with 'bout anything else. Roy was always lookin' to help out, and earn a few extree bucks. I had about 150 head of horses I was drivin'. Well, I knew I had several crippled after the wreck. I went over and called my boss in Jackson – the ol' gal from Boston that owned the Half Moon Ranch outfit – Miss Tarbell. 'I can be there in about two hours,' she told me. I told her, 'The railroad pens are just off to the right as you're comin' through Newdale. I'll be sittin' in the truck watchin' for you.'

Miss Tarbell got there, went and got a motel room, and then her and I went to supper. Hell, we'd, me, Roy and Eleanor, already had a fire a goin'. We was fixin' to cook-up some hamburgers, and were plannin' to bed down right there at the railroad pens – like we did in Victor on our first night's stop in Idaho on the drive.

Miss Tarbell asked me if I knew what horses we'd had to put down. Naturally I did. I named a couple and she started to cry. I said it was startin' to get dark, shortly after the accident and, I didn't remember the other two. I'd lied to keep Miss Tarbell from getting any more upset. She'd raised most of them horses in the herd and was pretty attached to each one of them. I'd put down two horses that were 17-years-old and had carried dude kids 14 years. You don't get 'em any better than that. And that was the same type of horses as among the ones that got all banged up.

Miss Tarbell could hardly eat, upset over all those horses, and how she'd raised them. She asked how much that was goin' to set us back on horses for next summer.

'I don't know. Are we booked plum full for camp again?'

'Well, yes, we're a little more than that. We're more than this summer. I got four more girls than we'd had. This year we had 46.'

They kinda hog-tied me out there, at the scene of the accident, waitin' on the Highway Patrol, while Eleanor and Roy put the horses in the pen. You couldn't shoot 'em - euthanize the horses until the authorities got there. I had the rifle and shells. When someone finally got there the patrolman said,

'I'll shoot 'em.'

'No, you won't! I'll shoot 'em myself and know damn well it'll take one shot.'And that's what it took. He wouldn't know where to shoot a horse to put it out quickly and painlessly. Every time I touched that gun he said,

'Watch where you're shootin! Watch where you're shootin'!'

He did every damn thing he could think of a way to ball me up. And I killed them all with one shot. I don't know what he was belly-achin' about. He was just mad cuz he didn't get to target practice. He tried to find anything to pick at.

'Sooner or later you'll get a chance to tell your story,' I told the farmer. Anyway, I offered to settle with him before I called Miss Tarbell. I was goin' to settle for the four head and I hadn't even seen the others yet. It was damn lucky he didn't go along cuz I was goin' to settle on the four head for $1,000 - $250 a head.

'Well they're not worth that kinda money."

He didn't know a damn thing what I was doin' with the horses, or about their type of life. I didn't say no more. It was too dark and I was too tired to get in an argument. At that time in my life, if I was right, I didn't care who I got in an argument with."

The Highway Patrol finished their report. Arrangements were made to haul away the dead horses. The farmer got ticketed for careless and reckless driving. After an assessment was made of the remainder of the herd, Miss Tarbell eventually settled with the farmer. Grant completed his trek with the herd to their winter range - where they would graze until the next summer. In late May, or early June, of the following year, Grant would trail the horses back to the Half Moon Ranch from Idaho.

A Half Moon Ranch saddle horse, ca. 1950.

The Log Cabin Bar in downtown Jackson Hole about 1950.

Chapter Seventeen

THE LOG CABIN BAR

The favorite watering hole for the cowboys, ranch hands, and dude wranglers in Jackson Hole back in the '50s and '60s was the Log Cabin Bar. Back then it was located on the corner of Broadway and Cache on Jackson Square. In the '30s and '40s locals referred to it as the Log Cabin Club and it was a haven for gamblers. One could always find there a rousing game of poker, blackjack, craps, or roulette to join in on. It was also the place of choice for locals to vent. More than one unfortunate found his way out of the bar through the plate glass windows on the front of the club.

If it was excitement you were chasing in Jackson, there was no better place to find it particularly on Saturday nights, after the rodeo. The Log Cabin played a special role during Grant Beck's Jackson tenure. It was at this bar where he had his first town fight, where he traded his boots for the Two Bar Spear brand – and later walked out of the bar in his stocking feet, and where he occasionally stopped by to find an extra hand for the Half Moon Ranch.

> *"Hell," said Grant, "I went to town every Saturday night just like everybody else. I was single tryin' to get double."*

It was a Saturday night before rodeo season, early June about 1955, when Grant dropped in the Log Cabin. He was the foreman at the Half Moon Ranch in Moose, WY, in his mid-twenties. Grant had been one of the youngest ranch foremen in the entire Jackson area. Like he often found himself at the start of the summer camp and pack season, Grant was short of help at the ranch. They had a bunch of horses that needed shod and needed to put some riding time on before the dude kids showed up. When Grant pulled up to the bar he noticed a vehicle not from around Jackson. Something about it drew his interest.

"It was a '37 or '38 Ford coupe. Had a saddle in the trunk. The trunk lid wouldn't shut all the way cuz the saddle stickin'-up, so its driver had it tied down with some rope. On the top of the trunk lid was tied his bed roll. Now, I knew that car belonged to a cowboy."

Grant strolled into the Log Cabin, bellied up to the bar, and ordered bourbon straight. Roy Ransom was tending bar that evening.

Grant Beck and Charlie Johnston working horses in 1955.

"Roy was a good kid. I'd knowed him purdy good. He worked a little for me in Jackson. He'd helped me trail horses over from Idaho when I had that wreck. Charlie Johnston, owner of the Ford coupe, saddle, and bed roll that was outside the bar, come over near to where I was talkin' to Roy. I told Roy, 'If he runs out of money, why, give him a drink. Write it down somewhere, but don't tell him I bought it or nothin'."

Sure enough Grant noticed Charlie digging in his pockets.

'Give that ol' boy a drink down there,' I hollered at Roy. Roy walked down to the bar where Charlie had pulled up a bar stool,

'You need a drink?'

Gosh, he'd spent $25 or $30 in there in no time – buyin drinks for himself and any fool at the bar.

'I think I've about had it,' Charlie said to Roy.

I seen him down there a fishin' in his pockets – he didn't have a damn penny left.

'Let the outfit buy you one,' Roy said.

Then Roy served him a drink on me. Charlie come down and sit right next to me and started talkin' about a job. I told him I had one and I all knowed about it – what was expected of the position and such. I asked if he could shoe a horse. That was my biggest worry.

'Yeah, I'm not fast,' Charlie said. Anyway, he said he'd follow me home to the Half Moon.

'Well, when do you wanna go, Charlie?' Grant asked.

'It won't be very long. I'm gonna go out to the car and sleep a bit.'

'Whadda ya call a bit?'

'Two hours.'

'Well, drink up and then I'll wake you in two hours.'

Charlie Johnston on Butte, 1955, with Grant Beck standing by ready to lend a hand.

Two hours come along. Christ, it was 4:30 in the morning. The bars had all closed. I'd sit there and talked with Roy all this time. Roy said to me,

'You gonna hire him? You gonna hire that drunk?'

'I already hired him.'

'You must be hard up for help.'

'Christ, I'm all alone, I oughta be!'

So I hired ol' Charlie, and this is after I trailed horses over from Idaho. Yeah, I was 26, cuz I was married to Eleanor. And that's when I had my tonsils out – on the third of June – after I trailed some horses over from Pinedale.

Charlie was 51-years-old when I hired him. I was 26. Anyway, I went out and woke him up. The café run all night back then, the café the Log Cabin had. I got him a cup of coffee. His car was just as full as it could be. I noticed he'd had a purdy fancy bridle and reins – stuff like that. I'd felt I really found a cowboy – a hand. By God, I did too!

The next day I showed him what I could, drivin' around in the pick up truck, and what to look for in these horses. Showed him where our summer range was and asked him if he could ride out there and get a count on what we had - a head count of the horses and which ones needed shod. And he did. I believe Charlie was the best man I ever hired at the Half Moon."

The Log Cabin Bar that Grant knew is long gone. There's a Coldwater Creek women's fashion store in its stead. Lou Gill had owned the bar back when it was called the Log Cabin Club, and when gambling was big at the Log Cabin, the Wort Hotel, the Cowboy Bar, and the RJ Bar. Lou Gill sold the bar to Lee Hill, who later sold it to Tex Randall and Jess and John Wort. Dick Boyer, John Wort's son-in-law, married to Lila, – Skippy Wort, and later bought Tex out. Then Tom Skeoch bought out the Wort-Boyer partnership, and moved the liquor license next door to the Rancher Bar. The Log Cabin Saloon, and the original license, is now located just outside of town on North Cache near Flat Creek. It is operated today by Tom Skeoch's son's wife's family. It's just not the same now as it was in earlier days.

An interior view of the Log Cabin Bar.

As for Charlie Johnston, he was one of the best hands, best all 'round cowboys Grant ever worked with. Charlie ended up marrying a counselor at the Half Moon – Harriet "Hickey" Clarke. Hickey was a professor at Radcliffe College. You can read Charlie and Hickey's story in Diane Koos Gentry's book – *Enduring Women*. When I read it, it sure reminded me a lot of my good friends Grant and Abie Beck. Abie, Grant's third wife, has a great many similarities to Hickey. Abie has become as much what the Two Bar Spear represents to its guests over the past 20 years as Grant is.

Jackson Square around 1950 with the ski slopes in the background.

Lee Gilbert on Cocky with Polly grazing beside him.

Chapter Eighteen

ROOTIN'
FOR THE RUNT

Courtesy of Lee Gilbert

It was a long dusty ride from Rock Springs to Jackson in one of those old Union Pacific stretched cars. Lee Gilbert was just eleven-years-old back in 1954 and about to embark on a new chapter in his life. His older brother had been sent out to the Half Moon Ranch in Moose, WY, from their Pennsylvania home the year before. The prospect of spending the summer at a dude ranch around a bunch of horses did not exactly excite this particular young easterner. In fact his only previous experiences with horses did nothing to endear the beasts to him. Both episodes involved runaways that, although left him physically unhurt, greatly diminished any desire to pursue horse riding as a pastime.

Grant Beck was the lead cowboy in charge of all of the Half Moon riding stock. In addition to breaking and training the ranch's young horses, Grant supervised irrigation and all of the field work. But for young boys and girls coming west for the first time, Grant's most important role at the Half Moon was placing them on the right mount – matching kid to horse or vice versa. It sounds easy enough, but consider what's at risk. When you're about four feet tall and 70 pounds or so, the prospects of climbing aboard a 15-hand, 1,100 pound animal is not the most natural or inviting thing to do, especially if you'd grown up in an environment where horses weren't a part of your daily, weekly, or monthly routine. In Grant's mind, he wanted to put each of his young charges in the position to have the most safe and rewarding experience. Grant loved and respected horses and he took it upon himself to give every person the best chance of coming away from a horse and riding experience feeling the same way. Grant's biggest challenge, even fear, was something happening in his realm of responsibility that would cause the natural fear most novices already have around horses to escalate.

For 50-some years Grant has successfully matched rider to steed thousands of times. It's truly an art. Grant is one of the cowboy/dude coach grand masters. For kids like young Lee Gilbert it made all the difference in the world.

"Grant put me on Ginger, a kind and gentle horse 20-some years old. He taught me how to steer, walk, trot, lope, and most important to me at the time – to stop. Because Ginger was obviously the right choice for me and my level of ability, I was able to do precisely what Grant instructed me to. In return, Grant built my confidence by heaping praise upon me. At that time in my youth, having anyone compliment or encourage me on anything was kind of foreign. At home it seemed I could never do anything good enough – probably my viewpoint as the middle child. But it was different at the Half Moon thanks to Grant."

Half Moon dude boys horsing around near the corral in 1955.

It's always Grant's goal to advance a young rider as quickly as his skills or the discipline dictated. As people do, horses too have their special skills. At the Half Moon Ranch in '54, as it would be on Grant's own Two Bar Spear Ranch later, the camp kids were groomed in horsemanship for two to three weeks in order to be prepared for a pack trip on horseback into the mountain wilderness. This made the pairing of horse to camper even more critical. The pack trip would equally challenge the ability and endurance of both.

"Ginger was the perfect horse to get schooled on. She wasn't sturdy enough for a wilderness pack trip. So Grant was going to put me on Cocky – might as well have been named Thunderbolt or Lightning. He was a huge sorrel horse, young and lively looking, and much too spirited to my way of thinking. Worse yet, Grant wasn't going to accompany us on the trip – it would be the Half Moon counselor and a wrangler.

Nonetheless, Grant put me on Cocky a couple days before our high country trip. As I would later learn to both expect and respect, Grant got me going on Cocky, as he always did with his young protégés, with the perfect combination of instruction and praise. Grant had sufficiently raised my confidence in Cocky and my own riding ability to ready me for the rugged three weeks ahead. Three weeks packing out on horseback in the Wyoming wilderness, sans the "space age" accoutrements and niceties available today, would build your confidence in a horse or make you miserable. Cocky was rock solid, just as Grant said he would be. He wasn't the least bit jumpy or nervous regardless of the challenges of the trail or inexperience of his passenger. By the time we had returned to the ranch, I'd ridden through hail storms, crossed swollen creeks, ridden over great burn areas, and crossed back and forth over the Continental Divide.

My feeling for horses had transformed from fear to a genuine respect and appreciation. My horsemanship had been elevated from both hands clutching on to the saddle horn with heart in mouth, bouncing uncontrollably in the saddle, to easily gripping with my legs, hands free and soaring like an eagle.

I couldn't wait to return home. Grant's rootin' for the runt had provided me with a new identity – one that has helped mold me into who I am today. Fifty years later I retain a sense of self – 'cowboy confidence' - that I will carry to my grave."

Lee Gilbert on Jasper.

Chapter Nineteen

A HOLLYWOOD DUST STORM

It was 1955 and the end of the summer pack season at the Half Moon Ranch. Hollywood once again had invaded the relative quiet of Jackson Hole. Director Rudolph Mate had chosen the scenic Snake River area near Moose Junction - just north of Jackson, near Deadman's Bar and Jackson Lake - as the backdrop for his fictional version of the historic Lewis and Clark expedition. The movie was loosely adapted from a novel by Della Gould Emmons. Charlton Heston portrays William Clark who is at odds throughout the movie with his partner Meriwether Lewis played by Fred MacMurray. Vying for the affection of Sacajawea (Donna Reed), the Indian guide who aided the real life adventurers, is one of the many plots in the movie that fuels the turmoil between the two explorers.

The film went through a series of name changes prior to its 1955 release. The first title was *Blue Horizons* which was changed to *Two Captains West* sometime during shooting of the film. The movie was actually released as *Far Horizons*, but was re-released in 1961 as *The Untamed West*.

The captivating scenery in this portion of Wyoming was neither the ideal nor an authentic backdrop. The impregnable wilderness was not a plausible place to have ventured on river boats. It did, however, present a host of never-ending challenges for the re-enacting Discovery team including hostile Indian attacks, hazardous river crossings, unscalable mountains, and the unpredictably harsh nature of the seasonal weather in the northwest. In the movie these elements served as intermittent diversions from the ongoing feud of the two lead characters.

Lee Gilbert, Grant Beck's very first "dude" boy, was all of 12 at the time. Grant was driving about 40 head of horses back to the Half Moon Ranch from the packing corral where they initiated their pack trips up into high country. Lee was the one young camper Grant had really taken a personal – almost fatherly – interest in. He was not just along for the ride, but expected to help with the drive. Grant has always known when to place the right amount of responsibility and expectations on his young charges. By giving young people tasks that seemed to demand a maturity beyond their years, he helped kids grow up, learning something about horses and themselves, and in the process, feeling good about their accomplishments.

Lee was going to be at the head of the herd – a beacon for the horses to follow back to the Half Moon. Grant, along with Charlie Johnston, would bring up the rear keeping the horses grouped together and moving in the right, homeward direction. Unbeknown to the three of them, they were headed through a picturesque valley below the Grand Tetons along the Snake River, where a scene had been set up for the movie. Actors in Indian makeup and dress were scattered throughout the mountain forest, hiding in trees and surrounding their intended trail back to the ranch.

> *"One over there, one in a tree, and another one over there, scattered all over the place. Well, we didn't know we was ridin' through a movie set. Lee saw these Indians, not realizing they was actors, got scared, and kicked in to his horse's flanks. Well, he took off at a gallop with all 40 head racin' behind him. It was dry on the trail. It weren't long before the whole bunch of them was enveloped in a cloud of dust. Couldn't see a thing! We was only about five miles from the gate. Lee got to the corral first and got the gate poles kicked through the log fence posts. The herd went right in where they were supposed to. Charlie and I was comin' up the trail from behind the dust cloud. Couldn't see a damn thing. There was a jeep chasin' me from behind - a cloud of dust in the front and one in the back. When Charlie and I got to the gate, I halted our horses to confront Lee. It weren't long before the dust cloud trailin' us caught up. All of a sudden the three of us were surrounded by these Hollywood folks. Some guy jumped out of the front seat and yelled, 'Ya know what you just did? You wrecked a whole day's shoot!' I'd been wonderin' what'd got into Lee and that herd. Now I knew. Guess that was live action but didn't follow too close to their script."*

Reminiscing about that day's storied events, almost 50 years later, Lee offered the following in his defense.

> *"This was a particularly hot, dusty, late August afternoon. It took several hours ride from the corral to get to the Snake River crossing on a long causeway-type bridge. Having trotted the horses for most of the afternoon along the flat sagebrush prairie, fairly uneventfully, we came to a long timbered island. It was comprised of a stand of tall, lodgepole pine trees on a*

low rise. This island was several miles long and about a half mile wide. Cutting across the island was the shortest, quickest distance to the ranch located on the other side.

Now, you have to remember that this was 1955 – when cowboys were the good guys and Indians were the savages. At least that's how it was portrayed in the movies, and stamped into my subconscious. And it helps to remember that back then a 12-year-old boy without the influence of TV, computers, or a Game Boy – just his imagination – was easily influenced by what he saw on the silver screen.

As lead rider, it was my job to lead the herd across the river, find the cut through the timber island, and guide the horses through the trees to the other side. Not long after Jasper – the horse I was riding – and I entered the island along a very narrow trail, the trees and bushes seemed to close in around us. Except for the muffled clapping of horses' hooves on the hard-packed trail, and their continual labored snorting, the forest was eerily quite. Suddenly Jasper's ears perked forward and his head jerked up. He furtively glanced side-to-side. Jasper's gait became somewhat hesitant – almost erratic. The hair on the back of my neck crept up and I felt as if there were a 1,000 pairs of menacing eyes peering down upon me. Then I saw something that made my blood run cold: off to the right, just off the trail and barely visible, peeking through a bush ominously at me was an Indian in full war paint – bow, quiver of arrows, and knife. I could hardly – didn't want to believe it. As the horror of my situation sunk in, more and more Indians revealed themselves to me, hiding behind tress, bushes, rocks, whatever, all in war paint, grim and threatening. Impulsively, I grabbed hold of Jasper's reins and with both hands pulled myself low onto his neck. Instinctively - without hesitation – Jasper launched into a full gallop, racing straight ahead, crashing through the timber. That's all the encouragement that was needed from the following herd as they hastened to keep stride. As we burst through to the open sage prairie, on the other side of the pine grove, distancing ourselves from the imminent danger, the string of horses surrounded Jasper and me as we gradually slowed our maddening pace.

Grant and Charlie galloped up mad as hornets, berating me for pushing a weary string of horses like that through a treacherous stand of timber. Still in shock, and clearly without my wits, I managed to mumble something about Indians, a war party, and running for my life. Due to the blinding dust cloud we'd stirred off the trail, Grant and Charlie were confused by my story. Their upset with me seemed on the verge of anger when off in the distance, a smaller cloud of dust was trailing an oncoming jeep. As the jeep bounced through the sage toward us, it soon became obvious that Charlie and Grant weren't the only ones angry and upset. Tempers turned to laughter as I retold my story to Grant, Charlie and the director of a film crew. My youthful innocence and genuine fear must've been both engaging and convincing."

If you should happen to have the opportunity to watch *The Untamed West*, and in the course of the movie an inexplicable cloud of dust appears during an Indian ambush, just think about putting yourself in Lee's boots and stirrups and ask yourself what you might have done at the ripe old age of 12 years.

Horses going through a stand of timber at a much more normal pace.

Grant Beck shoeing a horse at the Half Moon Ranch pack-in corral around 1950. The corral was located above Turpin Meadow near Pacific Creek, above Jackson. Not shown in the picture are the two dude boys sitting on other end of the pole.

Chapter Twenty

COWBOY (DIS)TEMPER

Courtesy of Lee Gilbert

There wasn't a thing Grant Beck couldn't do around a ranch. This, of course, included doctoring a horse. On this particular occasion, Lee Gilbert wasn't sure just who would benefit from the inoculation.

"Grant really took to me and always found a way for me to help. When he was messing with one of the horses I typically found myself at the end of the lead rope attached to the horse's halter to hold his head still. It was no different when he was doling out shots. Grant would slap the horse's rump a couple-three times slipping the needle into the horses hide on the last slap thereby masking the stick of the needle. With the needle safely in, Grant would screw in the serum-loaded syringe to the needle protruding from the horse's butt and deliver the shot. Most horses took to this fairly routinely. Occasionally though, a horse would start to fuss and start throwing its head a bit making my job at the north end a bit more challenging. Grant didn't have much tolerance when his patients didn't act to his level of expectation. His temper wasn't one of those simmer-to-a-boil types, but more like a bolt of lightning. The suddenness in which he could explode frightened horse and helper alike and neither wanted to be the target of his fury.

It had been a long morning of Grant giving distemper shots. By mid-afternoon, following lunch, I suspect all of us – Doc Grant, me, and the horses were getting a little weary. Grant led up a docile mare and handed me the lead rope. I was focusing most of my attention on the horse and its head, secondarily on Grant's flurry of swats and needles. All of a sudden Grant cursed through clenched teeth. I was caught by surprise because the horse hadn't even flinched. When I peered around to assess the situation, I could see Grant's finger pinned to the horse's flank. He'd somehow got his finger between the needle and horse's rump and stuck himself. As my eyes grew to saucer-size, and my chin dropped to my chest, Grant handed me the syringe and proceeded to pull the needle out of the mare's derrière and back through his now-punctured and bleeding digit. He quietly pulled out his handkerchief, wrapped it tightly around his finger and went about the rest of his doctorin' like nothing happened.

Grant will always surprise you. And of course I was waiting for an explosion. After he finished with that mare he reached for the lead rope and looked at me with that smile in his eye and said,

'Guess I won't get distemper this year!'"

Grant Beck working young horses in the Half Moon Ranch corral, ca. 1950.

Chapter Twenty-One

EVERY DUDE BOY'S DREAM

Courtesy of Lee Gilbert

There is real significance in the following story told by Lee Gilbert. It speaks volumes of Grant Beck and the effect he's had on "his" kids, and folks in general that've had the occasion to be around Grant throughout his life in the West. It was true for me although I was 19 – when I went to work for him. I'd had the opportunity to do just what Lee had intended to. I know it was true for countless others as I have heard it first hand time and time again. Lee tells it with warmth and from the heart. Pull the log closer to the fire, pour yourself a cup of camp coffee, and try and imagine yourself in Lee Gilbert's shoes.

"In 1956, towards the end of my third year at the Half Moon, Grant approached me in confidence – me, a 13-year-old dude boy, and he one of my heroes. Grant shared his concern that Miss Tarbell had passed on some ownership of the Half Moon to a nephew. Grant wasn't at all comfortable with the proposed change of management and was concerned that the place would never be the same. Miss Tarbell had run the ranch for decades with a certain philosophy that Grant suspected her nephew didn't share. With Grant's ability to read people like he reads horses, I suspected he was right on. There was even talk of bringing electricity to the property. Grant shared with me that he'd purchased a ranch in the Pinedale area and intended to emulate what he liked most about the Half Moon operation. Then he dropped the bombshell – one of the most important questions ever directed my way: would I be the first camp counselor at his new ranch?

To appreciate how that offer made me feel, you have to understand how miserable I was away from the Half Moon and Grant. At home, I felt like a chunky, awkward-looking, scaredy-cat. My brothers, one older and one younger, were aggressive, exciting, over-achieving, handsome, blue-eyed wonders. My older sister – a girl – didn't count. As demanding as Grant was, and as fierce was his temper, when you succeeded in his eyes, you not only received praise, but new responsibilities – something I craved. Grant empowered me in every way. I always knew where I stood with Grant. He provided me confidence to where I felt there was nothing I couldn't do. What an incomparable feeling of worth that was for me. In just three years under Grant's tutelage, I'd gone from a terrified child on a horse, to a rootin', tootin' cowboy with a horse of my own.

Would I be Grant's first counselor at his Pinedale outfit? You bet your bippy! Not only did I accept Grant's offer, I asked him if he'd adopt me so I'd never have to go back East again. He'd said he'd be proud to. I was full of myself. So full in fact, I went back home and told my parents that after the coming school year, not only did I have a full-time job back in Wyoming, but that Grant Beck was willing to adopt me so they would no longer have to bother with me. I was never sent West again."

Lee Gilbert has been successful beyond all imagination. He and Grant share a bond of friendship I am fortunate to understand. All of us wish that our children grow up with the right role models. I can tell you matter-of-factly, as can Lee, how important Grant has been in our lives – past, present, and future. I have experienced the positive influence Grant has been on my eldest daughter, Heather. What is most amazing are the dozens and dozens of people who have been touched by this Wyoming cowboy, and his horses, in a similar fashion.

Grant Beck in the center of the photo taken sometime during the late 1970s. To the far right is George "Chopper" Grassel, IV. Chopper was working at the Two Bar Spear Ranch in a role similar to what Grant Beck offered Lee Gilbert.

Sherrif Olin Emery, center.

Grant Beck on Chip at the Two Bar Spear Ranch around 1979.

Chapter Twenty-Four

TIMES COULD BE TOUGH IN THE FEEDLOT

Courtesy of Eldon Ross

"Grant is a rare individual and certainly fits the picture of a Wyoming cowboy."

– Eldon Ross

Those are the words of one of Grant's oldest and closest friends. Eldon was 82-years-old when he sent me a letter that read as follows:

"Grant came to Idaho to winter, probably in the late '60's. He came with his Appaloosa horses and got himself a job at the local feed yard. He broke horses all winter by riding them in the feed yard sorting cattle. He doctored the sick cows and did just general all around work that needed done on horseback. At that time I ran a service station in Star, ID, where Grant lived and became a customer. I found Grant to be an honest, hard-working person. We gradually developed a friendship. I later sold my business and went into farming. I also had a small herd of Purebred Horned Hereford cattle. Grant eventually bought some ground in the area and I farmed his land for him for a number of years. In the winter he would buy some cattle if he hadn't already raised enough of them to expire the feed crop raised from his farm.

We had a fifty-fifty arrangement. I did the work and he furnished the land. We split the seed and fertilizer and whatever expenses were extra. We never had a written agreement. It was all done with a handshake and a pat on the shoulder or a nod of the head. In most cases we both fed off the same stock of feed and kept track of our own usage. As far as I know, we never felt like either of us was being cheated of our fair share.

In the early spring, when we had those late storms and our cows would be calving, we would check on each others' cows through the night, taking turns every two hours. We would look after our own until about 10:00 p.m. and then alternate every couple hours to make sure no new calves would drown in a water hole or freeze to the ground.

I always kept up to a half dozen horses for him through the summer months and he always paid me well for their keep.

My wife and I have spent quite a bit of time at Grant's ranch in Pinedale, and his hunting camp above the Gros Ventre. He would never accept any money for this. One summer we went on the kids' June pack trip. We came back down the mountains just in time for the Green River Rendezvous and Pinedale Rodeo.

My wife died in October of 1986. Grant and Abie drove 1,000-miles roundtrip to attend the funeral and for Grant to be one of her pallbearers.

Grant and Abie have also known that anytime they are in our part of the world there is food and a bed waiting for them. In June of 1999, Grant drove 1,000 miles in one day to come to my 80th birthday party. They drove 500 miles each way and stayed and visited for only an hour. They got back to the ranch just in time to take out a pack trip the next day.

My wife once told me that all my friends were strong willed, opinionated, and had a mind of their own. Everything had to be fair and honest or I wouldn't have anything to do with them. As I thought that over, I considered it a compliment because if you don't have the conviction you are doing things right, it's time to change. Grant is my friend."

Eldon Ross on Chip and his wife Donna on Bud.

Two Bar Spear Ranch pack trip guests heading out for a day trip from a Bridger Wilderness camp site near Freemont Crossing.

Chapter Twenty-Five

HE CAN RIDE A HORSE, BUT CAN HE HOLD A TUNE?

Courtesy of Donna Sievers

Donna Sievers echoes the sentiments of many folks when she writes, "Grant is certainly one-of-a-kind and we consider him a dear friend." Donna and Bob Sievers moved to Pinedale in 1951. They became acquainted with Grant and his first wife Ellie through a young married couples group at a local church. Grant and Bob frequently could be found jawing over a pool match at one of Pinedale's local bars. Donna even claims to have gotten her first mare from Grant as the result of winning a wager during a pool match. Coming from Grant, you can bet it was a good mare. Among Donna's recollections, and contributions to *Camp Coffee*, is something only a lucky few witnessed – Grant's singing. The Sievers went on a number of pack trips over the years with Grant, and accordingly, Grant had no small role in Donna's love for the mountains. "Grant and Abie were great hosts and his tales and songs around the campfire, under the stars, always contributed to the fun."

Packing through the Wind River mountain range on enough occasions, one can relate to chilly, wet day trips from base camp, like the one Donna refers to in her story at Summit Lake. To keep the fire burning and keep everyone warm throughout the evening Grant would take off on horseback, lariat rope in hand, and often times return dragging a huge tree stump right into the open fire. Grant's well deserved reward was always a hot cup of camp coffee. The recompense for those anxiously awaiting Grant's return was another of his tales and evidently, on a rarer occasion, even a song.

> *"On one trip to Clear Creek we came in from a cold, wet ride and, as usual, Grant built up a fire and put on his famous coffee pot. It had been an abnormally dry year in the Bridger Wilderness. Subsequently, the Forest Service had banned all fires in the area that season. This*

day had been unusually wet and cold. In an effort to take a bite out of our chill, we were, albeit in violation of the ban, enjoying a warm fire and hot coffee. Grant would have had it no other way. He's always been sensible and especially hospitable. Along came a Forest Service ranger. My first thought was how much the fine would be. Grant never hesitated inviting the official into camp for coffee. The appreciative ranger warmed up and sat a spell before moving on. No comments were ever made with regards to the fire. A warm fire under inclement weather conditions would go a long way in preventing guests from getting pneumonia, but a fire ban is the law. It must have been obvious to the Forest Service representative that Grant was just trying to use good sense. That is a testimony to how Grant has always been viewed by local authorities: be it the Forest Service, the Fish and Game, or any one of the local law enforcement agencies."

Donna tells:

"Another time we'd fished at Borum Lake and were loading up to go back to camp. Some young men approached on foot, one of them using his climbing stick as a crutch. He claimed to have broken his ankle. Dr. Yednick, a local Pinedale physician, was conveniently on our pack trip and checked out the ankle. The hiker wanted one of our horses to ride out on, but we had no extras. Dr. Yednick assured everyone that nothing was broken. Grant declined on forfeiting one of our mounts. A discussion ensued and several of us agreed to trade off walking and riding thereby letting the injured hiker borrow a horse. Before any conclusion could be made Grant took off on foot up the trail – at a lope – forfeiting his own mount to the injured hiker. We thought we'd catch him, all of us being on horseback. We never did. The fire was going and the camp coffee percolating when we reached camp."

"A typical day found Grant on his back, hat over his eyes, dozing after we were all set up to fish."

This is an image that all of us who have shared time with Grant in high county have a vivid recollection of.

"Another time," Donna shares, "the horses took off on their own and early morning saw

Grant heading towards Crows' Nest in hot pursuit. We stayed put at camp and had breakfast. Before long here comes Grant, blood running down his face, leading the rest of the horses. He'd ridden head-first into a branch, puncturing his forehead, and knocking him off his horse – no small feat for that cowboy! A cup of camp coffee, spiked with a shot of Jack Daniels, and not a complaint from him. Lean and tough!"

Grant sang at Bob and Donna's 50th wedding anniversary. It is rare that Grant misses a close friend's special occasion, and even rarer still that he doesn't make some spur-of-the-moment contribution that adds to the memories. What did he sing? Donna couldn't recall but suggested a couple past favorites from his known repertoire: "Does the Spearmint Lose Its Flavor In the Bed Pan Over Night?" or, "I've Got Tears In My Ears."

Grant Beck on Brew dragging a log to the camp for the campfire at the Clear Creek camp site.

Leif Lie with Scarlet to the left, and the author's mount – King – near hunting camp above the Gros Vente River outside Kelly, WY, ca. 1980.

Chapter Twenty-Six

HE WEREN'T A GREENHORN

Stepping into the real West for the first time, dandified by city life, indifferent to western ranching customs, easterners often find themselves labeled "greenhorn." Not that a particular individual doesn't know anything, but the moniker does suggest that western life is a rather foreign thing. One just doesn't quite seem to fit. For the most part, non-westerners' notions of the "cowboy code" originates from what Hollywood producers project on to the silver screen. The objective for all western newcomers and visitors, including myself in 1976, is to shed the "greenhorn" label as quickly as possible. Acceptance is important. We're all prideful. Fitting-in, or being accepted and respected by locals, entails proving one's worth. This right of passage can only be accomplished through actions – especially not words.

Life in Wyoming is typically simple, but hard. One's actions are one's reputation. In a town like Pinedale, you may not know anyone after the first couple of weeks, but believe me, they know you. At the very least, the locals know of you. Early impressions are everything. Not much hay grows under one's feet before you get the sense of belonging, or the sense that you might just as well move down the road.

I always look back on when I bought my first horse. As much as I resisted the notion, I was a "greenhorn." Just as green as the horse I bought from Grant. We made a pact, that gelding and I. We were going to lose that green label together. Eventually we did. No worse for the wear, I might add.

Leif Lie was no "greenhorn." He may have been one of those rare individuals who, by their nature, never were "greenhorns" – like Grant Beck. But Leif and Grant did not travel the same road to get there.

I met Leif at Grant's hunting camp in the fall of 1976. By that time Leif had been a regular in camp pretty much without exception for the prior 13 years. Leif was 61-years-old that fall. My first impression of him was that I'd never before met anyone with his stamina, regardless of age. Although in respectable condition myself, with youth weighing heavily on my side, in the mountain draws and valleys of the Bridger Wilderness outside of Kelly, WY, in the Gros Ventre, I was no match for Leif. It just might have been Leif who they modeled the energizer bunny after. As I learned over the years, there was much more to the man than his boundless amount of energy.

It's been said that a person's worth, or greatness, is measured by the friends one keeps. I believe that. I also deem the same can be said when measuring the qualities of a person by those who choose to be around him or work for him. Employees or associates need not necessarily be friends. But they can certainly play a role in defining who each of us is. Leif wasn't formally Grant's employee. He was never paid nor expected payment. Over a span of about 25 years he showed up nearly every fall to cook, wrangle, and guide at Grant's hunting camp. That's a testament to them both.

Leif was born in 1915. He was one of nine children born in a Minnesota farming community. His common sense, practicality, and work effort had a lot to do with having spent summers and after school working as a farm hand. In 1940 he graduated from the University of Minnesota where he had wrestled in the 128-pound-weight class on that college's team. Shortly following graduation, he joined the Navy. Leif set his sights on being a pilot. He learned to fly the Navy's seaplane. Later Leif became an instructor. In 1943 he was the squadron leader for a Navy seaplane unit stationed in the Aleutian Islands throughout World War II. It was 1950 before Leif's tenure of service in the Navy had expired.

Leif Lie standing by his truck parked near hunting camp, with the majestic Grand Tetons in the background, ca. 1980.

Leif had demonstrated his leadership ability throughout his Naval career by mentoring the young men under his command. Even more to his credit was the influence he had in directing young men towards manhood during 35 years as a wrestling coach back home in Minnesota. It's no small wonder that he adapted so well to the outdoors. To witness him in action in the Bridger Wilderness one could appreciate someone who's truly in his element.

It was 1963 when Leif came across an advertisement for Grant Beck's hunting services under a Wyoming outfitter's listing. The ad itself was a rarity as Grant built his 50-year-plus business almost entirely on word-of-mouth referrals. Leif was looking for a hunting experience that was also connected to a working ranch. Grant's operation sounded ideal. Grant invited him along for a pack trip he had planned in August of that year. If Grant had any ulterior motives, Leif was none the wiser.

Grant's uncanny ability in recognizing qualities and traits in people – the same as horses – applied with his instincts about Leif. I'm sure his phone conversations with Leif interested him beyond just needing another hunter in camp. Grant was always looking for good help. A group of Rocky Mountain Big Horn Sheep hunters from Colorado had booked a hunting pack trip with Grant. Leif had been invited to "tag" along. It was a half-day ride in the Bridger Wilderness, a stop by Marm's Lake, before Leif realized he was the official cook of this expedition. Although it may have come as a surprise, you can bet Leif was up to the task. These hunters may not bag their sheep, but, by golly, they'd eat as well on the trail in high country as anyone could expect.

I've always wanted to go on a sheep hunt. I'm not sure if I would actually follow through with harvesting one. But, I yearn for the challenge of getting close enough to a legal ram – horns with a minimum of three-quarters curl – to make the choice. Obtaining a sheep permit in Wyoming is a chore in itself. Even residents have to apply to be drawn for a permit. I've known Wyoming residents who have failed to draw a license in 30 years of applying.

Grant claims that Pinedale longtime resident Les Anderson was the best sheep hunter he ever knew. Grant and I frequented the restaurant at Pinedale's VFW and I used to sit around and be mesmerized during Grant's and Les' exchange of tales.

Mark Stockton of Dubois, WY, was another accomplished sheep hunter. He was a onetime partner in the Triangle R Outfitter's of Pinedale with Larry Vance and Rusty Gouch. Mark's shared some of his sheep hunting experiences with me.

Sheep hunting in Wyoming's Wind River Range is not for the faint of heart. It is easily the most physically and mentally demanding hunt of all of Wyoming's big game. While most of the action takes place above timberline, it is no small task getting there. Following a long day's ride in on horseback, and setting up camp, being successful generally means forfeiting the horses for a foot climb among the rocky precipices. Often times a second camp – a spike camp – is required close to where you can spend hours with binoculars glassing the canyons for a sighting of this most elusive prey. If a legal ram is spotted, there is only a slight chance that you can figure a way out to climb to a position where you might be offered a shot. Getting in position to fire a shot might be a half-day's proposition. Imagine if you get within 200-300 yards of your target, are lucky enough to get a shot off, and are expert enough marksman to be successful. Getting to your downed quarry, field dressing the sheep, quartering it and hauling it out might take a couple to a few more days. The head, horns and cape alone could way 75 pounds. And, remember, you left the pack horses at base camp. Yet, I still yearn to go on a sheep hunt.

While Grant, Leif, and the Colorado hunters sighted some sheep, they were never in a position to harvest any. But the trip wasn't a total loss. Grant had found the most dependable and competent help in Leif that he would ever have in his hunting operation. For Leif's part he found a place he could call home each fall. It is hard to imagine a more engrossing spot if one loved being in a mountain wilderness.

Leif's stamina is a matter of record for the hundreds of hunters who spent anytime with him on Gravel or Sheep Mountains. But what he is most famous for are his pancakes. Cooking in high country requires a special discipline. Preparing really good meals in less than ideal conditions is an art. Leif's pancakes were a masterpiece. I'm not sure if he has ever given out the recipe, but I know there are those of you readers who can taste what I'm talking about.

Grant regularly comments on how fortunate he's been in his life. Part of that fortune is the where and how he has been able to live it. Another part is the horses. The hundreds of horses he has raised that have provided safe, reliable, and, most importantly, rewarding rides for his guests. But maybe the biggest part is the people. All of those individuals that he has helped, guided, taught, nurtured and just plain encountered; those people that Grant has had an effect on; and those who have had an effect on him. Leif is among them, and has been now for 40 years. I am fortunate to have known them both.

When I caught up with Leif in the spring of 2002, at his log cabin home near Hill City, SD, in the heart of the Black Hills, we talked of old times. Although at 87, his body won't let him blaze through the wilderness anymore, his eyes revealed the passion for the memories. We spoke of Grant.

> *"I've never known anyone who could do more things with horses," Leif explained. "He taught me a lot about horses, and a lot about the wilderness. Grant has charisma, and a lot of people were drawn to him. But he wasn't easy to work around."*

I could only nod and agree.

High-country hot cakes.

Chapter Twenty-Seven

DASHIN' THROUGH THE SNOW

Views from the Two Bar Spear Ranch hunting camp.

Whether you are a fan of big game hunting or not, I think the Wyoming Game and Fish Department has done a remarkable job of managing the state's wild game. In an environment like Wyoming, with rancher, wildlife, and national parks trying to co-exist, you need to have a plan. Hunting is undoubtedly the best and most humane way to maintain a delicate balance. Additionally, hunting has always been a vital revenue source for the state. Thousands of Wyoming residents have depended upon hunting and fishing over the years for their livelihood. Game must be harvested. Even Teddy Roosevelt, possibly this country's greatest American conservationist, understood the importance in managing the equilibrium of the wild herds through hunting. Roosevelt may also have been one of this country's greatest sportsmen.

Grant Beck was honored not too many years back for 50 years as a Wyoming outfitter. Fifty years of guiding hunters and fishermen, dudes and campers, through the Jim Bridger Wilderness. And while doing so, making sure that these areas were left in their natural state – unspoiled, when each season came to an end. When Grant was toasted for his lifetime achievements as a Wyoming outfitter, the two recognitions that were of the most value to him, of the many cast his way, were his record on safety and as a caretaker. After all, the mountain wilderness areas around Pinedale and Jackson Hole are his home, and have been for over 50 years. Grant, like most of us, is proud of his home, proud to show it off. Every time he 'comes home' he wants it to be safe and clean – unblemished.

As one might expect, along with those 50 years came a lot of memories and some truly great stories, some unbelievable. An important thing to know about Grant's hunting operation through the years is that not all hunters were there just for the kill. Grant was lucky. His hunters wanted to enjoy the camaraderie of hunting camp and the serene beauty of its environs. Every season, especially fall and early winter, the Bridger Wilderness and the Tetons are awe-inspiring. When one finds themselves in those parts, the sheer grandeur is utterly overwhelming. It makes it difficult to understand exactly what our place is amongst it.

Leif Lie spent more days hunting with, and for, Grant than anybody. He recalls the time that he had a couple in hunting camp from Pennsylvania. Leif had tracked a mule deer through the Aspen thickets somewhere below Gravel Mountain, above hunting camp. Both husband and wife held permits. In this case, as more often than not, it was ladies first. When the deer had stopped to graze, the hunters still obscure to it, and the lady in position for a clean, safe shot, drew the majestic deer in her sights, and then quietly pulled off of it.

> *"I think I'll pass," she said. "I can shoot a deer when I get home. Let's go find some wildflowers!"*

That of course was music to Leif's ears as he was as much naturalist and outdoorsman, as hunter and guide. It also serves as a fine example of how Grant's guests will continually surprise you and, most often, in the most pleasant of ways.

Some of Grant's best stories through the years were related to elk hunters. For many, seeing an elk in the wild is as much the experience as actually bagging one. And although a successful hunt not always required attaining one's quarry, it certainly remains a major part of the experience for most hunters. Half Moon Mountain is viewable looking north from the Two Bar Spear Ranch. In the early days, 25 years ago or so, prior to that area being as accessible as it is now to four-wheel drive vehicles, it provided some really good hunting – lots of game. One side of the mountain was mostly barren, scattered boulders protruding from sparsely-distributed, low-growing sage brush. The opposite side, facing to the north, was a dense pine forest. The best game spotting typically occurred at either dawn or dusk when one was positioned just inside the tree line. This area was always good for mule deer, occasionally for antelope, and at one time, a fairly good place for elk – if you caught them migrating just at the right time of the year. The elks' movement was usually hard to predict. Migration is primarily weather-related. The worse the weather in high country, the sooner and more likely elk would occupy some favorite haunts on Half Moon Mountain.

This particular outing involved a group of elk hunters, late in the season, atop Half Moon Mountain. It wasn't the hunt itself that makes the story worth telling, as much as what took place afterwards. As much as the normal reader will find this wholly unbelievable, I know it to be true. First of all, Grant's stories, as engaging as they are, are always fact-based and rarely fancified or exaggerated. Secondly, I have personally experienced enough instances that push the limits of plausibility that I never even second guess the possibilities, especially as it pertains to Grant's Wyoming experiences.

Accompanying Grant that afternoon were three or four hunters, all having been successful in drawing elk tags for the Half Moon lake area. A golden rule of hunting, especially late in the season, is to always expect the unexpected. More often than not this had to do with weather. This instance was no exception. The hunting party had downed three elk. The sun had set, daylight rapidly diminishing. Snow had begun to fall and temperatures were plummeting. The elk carcasses needed to get down the mountain and back to the ranch, or to Pinedale's game locker. While a great majority of Grant's hunts involved horses and mules, both for riding and packing, this time all he had was his Chevy Suburban carry-all. The hunters had been transported to the mountain via truck and ascended the mountain on foot. The dilemma was how to get the elk down.

With more daylight the best option would have been to return to the ranch and retrieve trailer, pack mules, and one or two saddle horses. The downed elk's positions were inaccessible by vehicle. I know of no man who can physically haul an elk down the side of a mountain. In cases like this, the mother-of-all-invention usually lies in the combination of Grant's intuitiveness with his creativity. The way Grant figured, what he had going for him was a mostly snow-covered, steep decline fairly open to the road below with the exception of an occasional boulder. He had very few options, it was getting dark and he was getting cold. His hunters, less used to the harsh climate, were mostly just cold.

The elk had all been gutted. Grant instructed the hunters in helping him remove the heads and bottom of the legs as he explained the advantages of gravity as it pertained to the weight of an elk and a hunter on a slick surface. I'm sure they had no clue what Grant intended.

"So I got the hunters to help me get 'em started over the edge. And Rob Post was there. He was helpin' me that fall with some of my hunting. Rob rode one down - the other end of Half Moon Mountain. There's some pretty big boulders, it was lucky that I missed 'em all. I got in the rib cage of this one, had his front legs cut off, so I held on to the stubs. And I rode him down and I had another one tied to his hind legs following behind me. And I know, sometimes, I was going 10 mph. And these big old boulders were getting pretty close but I never did hit one. But Rob Post did. And he was kind of hangin', grippin' the sides of the rib cage, just sittin' in it. Back behind the ribs, had his feet just kind of braced in there, he was sittin' damn near right inside the elk. Gosh, he come along and he hit a boulder, it really lifted that elk. Somebody took the Suburban around, and come around the other side of the mountain, instead of going up the end. I had to make two loads of mine. We had to go up and get Rob out of the rocks. He run out of snow, and couldn't slide no more."

Rob was a little bruised and battered but essentially no worse for the wear. Grant had gotten the elk from point A to point B, bringing an exciting and far-fetched end to a snowy, blistery day. The hunters were soon able to thaw out in the warmth of the ranch's main cabin. For the rest of us, we were left with one of the more fantastic of Grant's elk hunting stories. Imagine hearing this tale told while gathered around a roaring fire and sipping a steaming cup of camp coffee.

Two Bar Spear gateway.

Chapter Twenty-Eight

ITALIAN COOKING

A black Cadillac sedan with Chicago license plates purposely entered the Two Bar Spear Ranch gateway. The car crept up the sloped dirt drive toward the main cabin, occasionally sliding off into a rut and bottoming-out. The ranch staff looked on with odd, quizzical expressions. After all, they'd never seen a vehicle of this stature on the county roads in Pinedale, WY. As the car eased to a stop, the four doors opened in an almost forced unison. Four dark-complexioned, well-groomed and overly-dressed men stepped out. They briefly hesitated before offering any type of salutations. After careful study of every detail of their surroundings, relaxed smiles slowly appeared replacing the quartet's grave countenances. Hands were soon extended with greetings and introductions immediately following. It was very difficult to understand due to the heavy accents.

Americans' fascination with the mob has endured for decades. Beginning with the real life story of Al Capone, Elliott Ness and his Untouchables, and fueled with Hollywood's interpretations of the facts mired in graphic violence and fiction of the ever-popular and critically-acclaimed *Godfather* trilogy, *Goodfellas* and others, our thirst for these tales seems never to be quenched. Just when it seemed ready to pass disregarded by the next generation, the trials and tribulations of the Gotti family rekindled our flame of curiosity. So it is no small wonder that when Nunzio Castellena from Chicago, along with his three comrades from Detroit, Ferdinando Vergilio, Antoine Voccia, and Garzio Aikabeda, stepped out of their Coupe de Ville, after arriving to the Two Bar Spear Ranch, the imaginations of all those on hand spun wildly out of control.

Think what one may have conjured up if witnessing the scene of this party's arrival, especially when their gun cases were unloaded from the trunk. To this day, neither Grant Beck, Leif Lie, nor the author knows what any of these gentlemen's real occupations were. I did reach Mr. Castellano on the phone from his Chicago home recently and he declined to comment on their Wyoming adventure or anything else for that matter. Of course, there could be several reasons for his decision not to talk to me. It may be that he just didn't remember the details of his elk hunting experiences. The trip may not have been particularly remarkable. But let's face it, the story is much more entertaining if the remote possibility exists that he was in the "family business", whether true or not.

Whatever the fours' origin or lot in life, this specific trip, of thousands in which Grant has participated during his 50-plus years as a Wyoming outfitter, was memorable both to him and to Leif. Leif especially remembers Nunzio Castellano as being,

> *"Not much of a hunter, but really a good-looking man – the finest-looking man I ever knew! Their last meal, they invited Grant and I to participate in it."*

Amongst the gear unloaded from the trunk of the Cadillac, most noticeable were not the fancy hunting rifles but the boxes of cooking utensils and bags of groceries. Although three meals a day were included in the price of the five-day hunt, these gentlemen insisted on cooking dinner for themselves. They dined alone. That is something that had never happened at the ranch or hunting camp up until then, nor since.

Very few things come as a surprise to Grant. So the cooking arrangement of his four hunters was taken in stride. Grant felt the last meal they prepared, one that he and Leif were invited to, was a real treat - probably the best family-style Italian meal he's ever been party to. Through the course of this group's entire hunt what Grant found most memorable, and to this day can't share without laughing, is what he didn't get to see.

A hunter on Taylor Maid in the Two Bar Spear hunting camp.

Out of the four elk licenses that were drawn by these hunters only one elk was actually harvested. In Grant's recollection, while it was not a trophy animal, it was a nice size bull elk. The four were incredibly ecstatic - gleeful. It was almost eerie. It was obvious that they had not given much thought to what they would do with a game animal if their hunt were successful. The local locker plant was deemed not an option. They wished to take their "trophy" back to Chicago – in its entirety! Of course the elk had been field-dressed. And the temperature in November is typically cool enough that the elk would not spoil on the drive back. But where were they going to put it?

The departure morning, following an evening of breaking bread with their hosts, Grant and Leif helped hoist the elk carcass atop their shiny black Coupe de Ville. They strung rope from each of the animal's extremities around and through every possible place you could loop it and tie it to the car: through the windows, around the bumpers, through the door handles – there was rope everywhere. When they finished, although the windows didn't quite shut all the way, it appeared they just might make it back without incident, albeit a tad chilly. Grant chuckles every time he conjures up the image of this Cadillac, elk, and rope-tying spectacle. As funny as it may have been, according to Grant, it could not have been nearly as hilarious as the look upon Illinois drivers' faces as the suspicious looking black sedan and its passengers motored through Chicago's downtown loop.

Kathleen Kyle on Sonny and Grant Beck with King in hunting camp. Kathleen had been a summer camp counselor who stayed on to help during hunting season, fall of 1979.

Chapter Twenty-Nine

THERE ARE NO ELEPHANTS IN WYOMING

Given time and the chance to delve back into his cavernous holding of mountain memories, Grant could come up with a story or anecdote for almost every horse he ever owned, or dude, camper, or hunter he ever put on one of them. And like the following tale of a hunter from Minnesota, there is rarely one good story – on its own – that pertains to any of them – Grant has a wicked memory!

"He was coming down the trail on Big Bertha.

'Grant, I'm sick.'

As we were riding down from Sheep Mountain he passed alongside a big tree and stopped. After I heard him moanin', I turned around and rode back to where he'd stopped. He had wrapped both arms around the tree, still sittin' in the saddle. Both he and Big Bertha were just standin' there leanin' agin it.

He's the same hunter who'd brought an elephant gun to huntin' camp. It was a .456 Sievers or somethin' like that. He'd never shot it and was afraid to. So I said, let me shoot it.

'See if you can hit that tree,' he says.

'Hell, anyone can hit the tree. Put your hat on it!'

Well, I braced myself cuz I knew it was gonna buck me. Blew that hat to hell!"

A group of riders on a pack trip, with Grant Beck in the foreground, bringing up the rear on a trail near Trapper Lake.

Chopper to the left and a dude boy watching as Grant Beck shoes Thunder near the pack-in corral in the late 1970s.

Chapter Thirty

HELICOPTERS AND HORSESHOERS

In the old days most good cowboys were pretty handy shoeing horses. Most didn't make it a fulltime occupation but it was sure cheaper shoeing your own stock than paying someone – particularly if you had a slew of horses. Grant did both. He always, up until recently, shoed his own horses. At 77, it's a bit too much of a chore now for Grant. And from time to time, throughout his cowboying and ranching days, he has supplemented his living by shoeing for others. His horseshoeing skills were instrumental in getting him hired on as foreman at the Half Moon Ranch in Moose, WY, in 1948. Grant was 22-years-old.

I shod one horse in my life. Horsehoeing is an art. Beyond being about as physically demanding as anything I ever attempted, the horse's health and well-being are critically at stake in the shoeing process. I have the utmost respect for good shoers. It is much more a rarity today for horse owners to do their own shoeing. Like most owners, I have no problem paying sixty bucks to a professional. Imagine weighing a half a ton, carrying a couple hundred pounds and walking for weeks with the wrong size shoes on. As many different tasks as horses are asked to perform, it is important to tailor the trimming and shoeing to the demand of the exercise. A horse can be irreparably damaged by bad shoeing.

One thing I found common in all horseshoers is their story telling. For the most part, they like talking about their experiences and not the uneventful ones. The tales are usually centered on either a horse or owner that they had problems with – sometimes both. Listening to their stories is a small price to pay for playing such an important role toward the care of one's horse.

I reckon Grant has shoed about as many horses as anyone I know. So, naturally, he has about as many horseshoeing stories as just about anyone – probably enough for another book.

"That time I got busted up shoein' horses. Got some ribs broke, one (rib) in my lung, one (rib) in my kidneys. I was havin' a hell of a time. Anyway, what had happened, I went to the

doctor's office, and he just felt me and said you jut got a bad bruise. So like a damn fool, I went back out and gathered up my tools, and I was gonna finish shoein' this horse. I was about done when a helicopter flew over – pretty low – a Forest Service helicopter. I just had the lead rope wrapped around the top pole in the corral, and he (the horse) flew back so fast he jerked that pole off. It hit me in the back. People were watchin' this. They'd seen it happen. They had a fancy house and was lookin' out the door. They never come down. When I was getting' up, I didn't look where I was at. I was between the horse and that pole. He (the horse) seen me move, why he flew back again and hit me with that pole again.

And it took me a little bit to get up. I got up. I got that horse untied from the pole and damn, I was a hurtin'. I went back and was gatherin' up my shoein' tools, and I felt something kind of wiggle. And so, I just went home. We didn't have very good chairs, just straight back chairs, and I leaned back, and geez (did it hurt).

I ended up with gangrene and they kept me in the hospital. The doctor had some kind of gadget that he could pull it, move it (my rib). A pair of tongs, my God, that was pretty rough. I went down in the ambulance. And then when I got over that, I had John come down in the pick-up and get me."

Chapter Thirty-One

BORN AGIN DUDE

Like so many young people that have experienced time with Grant Beck on his northwest Wyoming ranch, or in the Wind River Mountain Range on a pack trip, Steve returned as an adult. Unlike most of the kids exposed to Grant and his way of life, the time he spent out West did not appear to have any of the long-lasting attributes those of us who know Grant have come to expect from most of his camp attendees and ranch guests. And, as with most cases, no one tells about it better than Grant:

"Well, I had that ding-a-ling up there (in the Wind River Range on a pack trip) who got me on Cincinnati television. The thing about that trip was that he'd tried to tell me that the Lord sent him on the trip, and, that I charged too much.

'The Lord said it was $100 too much!"

'When you get home,' I said, 'and you run into the Lord, tell him to give you a hundred bucks!'

He was tryin' to take over the trip. One of those born-again Christians. He was an alcoholic and pretty much a blowhard. He'd weighed a lot when he come out. He'd divorced his first wife (who Grant had known from previous visits). She was a good one – head of the blood bank in Cincinnati - in the nursin' world. Steve was originally from Albuquerque. He'd brung a whole bunch of western clothes (with him on an earlier trip). I'd modeled 'em up in the hills. That's when the sheepskin coat'd come out that had the rawhide on the outside. I wore one of those. It'd had elbow pads. He did get my white mule team on TV back in Cincinnati.

Group on a pack trip resting above Godfried Lake.

Well, things had went bad for him. Probably cuz he's dishonest. He and his wife separated. I had some lady cookin.' The two of them were pretty lovey-dovey up on the pack trip. Every night he'd take over the conversation around the campfire, tryin' to preach to everyone. Born-again Christian – I believe the right word in his case is "aborted Christian."

"You know what's going to happen to you?' he said.

'No,' I said, 'I wouldn't be surprised at anything though.'

'You're gonna die with a millstone around your neck!'

"That was about the last he had to offer around the campfire (that night)."

'You eat like sin down here,' he'd say.

"Christ, it wasn't long 'til you'd get pretty sick of it (him)."

Steve had been on a pack trip with Grant when he was a ten-year-old kid, more than 20 years before. He'd also attended summer camp the year following his first pack trip.

"He got kicked in the knee on that trip – Old George, an Appaloosa gelding Grant had raised that I rode as a three-year-old the winter of 1978. George'd had his head in a bush chewing on some branches. We were gonna go for another ride. Steve had chewed tobacco at that time. He was only ten.

Steve'd really wanted to come to camp the year following his first pack trip. Kathleen Kyle was the head camp counselor at the Two Bar Spear Ranch in the late '70s' said he couldn't come to camp unless he quit chewin'. Well, he quit chewin' and I don't think he's chewed since.

But he'd got kicked pretty hard in the knee – I heard it! George'd had his head in this bush, and Steve 'd went up to him and threw his jean jacket over George's hind end. He'd seen me lay mine over my horse's rear, fold it, then roll it up. So, that's what he was going to do. This was at Twin Lakes. So I stayed in camp with him the next day. I forget who was with me wrangling, mighta been Sherer. (John Sherer worked for Grant several seasons after the author did.) *Anyway, I stayed in camp with Steve. He got himself a stick and started hobblin' over to the campfire about 10 o'clock in the mornin'.*

'I think I'll be able to ride tomorrow,' he said.

'Good,' I said, 'that would be good for it if it don't hurt no more.'

And he did start ridin' the next mornin' with us. Never did slow him down a bit.!"

Grant Beck leading two of the members of his four white mule string.

Grant Beck on Amigo helping Lori Patterson, a young camper, by snubbing her horse.

Chapter Thirty-Two

AMIGO

When it comes to the discussion of which horse was Grant Beck's favorite, well, there have just been too many good ones through the years to pick. Although not often at a loss for words, I think this one just might have Grant a bit stumped. But for Abie Beck, Grant's wife, soul mate, and companion for the last two decades, the choice is pretty clear.

> *"Who'd you think?" Grant queried Abie. "I'd have to say as far as our 20 years together Amigo is definitely top dog. Just cuz Grant did so much on him. You could put a little kid on him, turn him out in the yard, and he'd be fine, both horse and kid. I had a picture of Lee Gilbert's little girl, when she was five, and she was at the ranch. She was ridin' Amigo around in the corral holdin' a cat."*

Grant added:

> *"That horse he was the best one. You could do anything with him. Anyone could ride him. If you ever roped a cow in your life, you wouldn't get in trouble on him. Didn't matter what side you roped the calf on. And I never had a colt get away from me snubbin' it."*

Personally, I can lend some credibility to Abie's claim, having had the good fortune of riding Amigo. Then, I have ridden so many of Grant's horses and there are many I could be swayed to vote for. And there are the hundreds that Grant rode prior to me ever knowing him. One thing's for certain; he was always riding a horse that everybody wanted to buy.

Grant may have never even acquired Amigo had it not been for the foreman of Robert Redford's ranch:

"I traded a pair of working draft horses for four or six head – I can't remember. I ended up with 17 of them J. B. King horses. Catalina Clipper was one of those horses – the mother of J. B. Buckshot."

J.B. Buckshot was a yearling colt I traded Grant for. I showed him in halter as a yearling and in Western Pleasure as a three-year old.

"And, they tried to buy some from me, Robert Redford's trainer, in Boise. Had me haul 'em into this, they was havin' a horse show there. And Noel Skinner – I knew him, he's from Jackson – he ended up bein' Redford's horse trainer. And, I thought I just as well put a good price for them. I said $3,000 a piece. I had one, a pink roan, a pretty thing, a mare, and he said,

'Well that here mare, I am probably interested in her but not for $3,000. Whadda ya take for her?'

'It don't matter if you're not interested does it?'

'You son-of-a-bitch,' he says, 'you know me from Jackson Hole.'

He was calf ropin' when I was a pickin' up there."

Grant was a pick-up man for the Jackson rodeo.

"Winey son-of-a-gun. You know sloppy, swaggert, always belly-achin' about somethin' for know damn reason at all. I out-showed him a lot up there in that arena.

A good colt will grow different than one that's not bred as well. And the reason they will, the ones that aren't bred so good, their heads will grow, their legs will grow, separate times. And their head is always the thing that grows first. And these other colts grow together, every bit of 'em. That's what I think. I've only got to witness that a little bit."

"But, anyway, this roan horse that Robert Redford's hand turned down, I traded her and $1,000 for Amigo. Amigo come off the race track. I got him comin' into four. He wasn't a fast horse. Hell, he couldn't run fast enough to buy himself a pair of shoes from any winnings. He was on the track in California. But he was plenty fast enough in the ropin' arenas around Pinedale. I roped on him quite a while. I gave him to Laurie, our vet, when he got 22-years-old. He lasted about a year, and then he got cancer. I give her Taylor Maid when Amigo died. She lasted pretty good – she was 26 when she died. Taylor Maid got in a fight and broke her leg. Getting in a fight with another horse. Broke her stifle. Laurie had to put them both down. Hired a backhoe and buried them both."

One of the many times someone tried to buy a Two Bar Spear favorite, Grant had hauled some horses back East to sell. While back there at the seller's barn, Grant recalls an incident with a couple of his hands.

"They'd cross-tied 'em, and come at him with a saddle. Christ, the horse, he'd flew backwards and tore two of the boards clean out of the stall – had quite a wreck in that stable. Max come in to see what had happened. Fired both of 'em right on the spot. He'd called Abie and me and said he couldn't do anything with this colt of his. After I'd went back to get him (the colt), he'd told me what had happened.

We'd hauled him out on another load of horses from Pinedale. He'd turned that unruly colt out to pasture prior to the time when we'd got there. Abie would usually ride all the horses we'd brought out in the arena for Max so he could see that they was what we'd told 'em. The year Abie had hurt her back and couldn't ride, I had taken Amigo with me cuz I knew I could snub any of the young horses to him and they could put anyone they wanted to on the horses snubbed to Amigo without an incident. I'd told Max that's what I'd brought Amigo for.

'I'll help anybody you want ride them,' I said. 'No,' he says, "I think they'll be just like the rest of 'em (we've ever bought from you). But whadda ya' gotta have for that horse you're ridin'?'

'We don't sell them kind, Max!'"

The Cowboy Steakhouse was in the lower level of The Million Dollar Cowboy Bar in Jackson Hole.

Chapter Thirty-Three

BUT CAN YOU COOK?

Courtesy of Maureen Curley

I first met Grant Beck in August of 1973 when I was waitressing at the Cowboy Steak House in Jackson, WY. I had been in Jackson since I graduated from college in May. My life was in kind of a holding pattern until the ski season started in November. That summer was a bit disappointing; especially since I was doing the very same thing that I would have been doing back East – serving meals in a restaurant. I'd come to Wyoming looking for some new experience. My initial conversation with Grant started me down a path that was more in line with what I thought the West was all about.

The Cowboy Restaurant was open until 4:00 a.m. Grant walked in on the early morning side one night and immediately started up a friendly conversation with me. He talked about his ranch and his horses. But most importantly for me, Grant mentioned that he was in the need of a cook for his hunting camp that fall. Did I know anyone who could cook? I wanted to know from him if this person (cook) could ride all she wanted to. His favorable reply convinced me to offer my services. Of course, this was assuming that I could boil water and make a hamburger. If I could a cook, I was hired. Grant said he would pick me up in front of the Wort Hotel in two weeks.

During the next two weeks I started to get cold feet. I visited with a friend who had bragged about being a hunting camp cook for one season. After a little digging, I learned the truth – he did it for one week and said it was hell on earth. Great, I thought. I'd signed on with a total stranger to live in a tent in the mountains for three months and cook for 20 hunters. I didn't even like the idea of hunting. I was an advocate for gun control. True to my word, however, I stood in front of the Wort on the assigned day. A small group of friends, my moral support group, was there to see me off. They had even bought me a cowboy hat so I looked more the part.

The green and yellow Ford pick-up truck pulled to a stop. Grant jumped out, shook my hand, and helped me toss my bags in the back. It all happened so fast. I jumped in and suddenly remembered my friends. As I started to wave goodbye, Grant glanced over at them and remarked, "Damn long haireds." I realized then that I was about to enter a world that was quite different from the liberal Boston college one I had just left. For that, I was more than a little worried. What I didn't know was just how much I would learn from the cowboy sitting beside me or how Grant would affect my life.

Although from our political viewpoints Grant and I were miles apart, we had a number of things in common. First, we both loved to tell a good story – although his were much more colorful than mine. I actually think I perfected my story telling at his knee. He seemed to have lived three lifetimes and still had a positive attitude in spite of some very hard experiences. Second, we both genuinely loved horses. Not only did he love to ride but he also enjoyed just messing with the horses. During my first few weeks at the ranch, I watched him shoe dozens of horses. It was back-breaking work and I wasn't much help. Somehow I got the impression that he loved doing it. When we went to the county fair to show Katy, he was just as excited as I and the two young cowboys who went with us were. Grant nearly went along with our idea to sleep in the stalls with the horses the night before the competition to make sure no one sabotaged our chances!

Grant Beck and friend on a hunting trip.

Grant was a good man with a high sense of what is decent, fair and honorable. He also had huge respect for the outdoors and animals, both wild and domestic My favorite story that illustrates this concerns a certain group of hunters who arrived mid-season. There were about eight of them who drove out from Michigan and arrived expecting the hunting trip of a lifetime. The hunters were up the first day at the crack of dawn. They climbed aboard the horses with great enthusiasm. By the end of that day they could hardly walk - a direct result of not listening to Grant and getting off to exercise now and then. From the beginning, they were pretty demanding. Grant kept checking-in with me on how I was being treated. As the week went on they became more difficult. Grant and I just kind of played it cool and didn't let it bother us.

On the fourth day, they left camp on horseback to begin that day's hunt. After a couple of hours they'd heard a rustle in the brush. When a porcupine innocently ambled out, one of the hunters shot him with a .357 magnum.

Grant stopped in his tracks and angrily asked the man why he did it. The hunter replied "That's the first thing I've seen moving since I got here." Right then Grant turned around and led them all back to camp never saying a word. When they arrived, he gave them all their money back and told them to get out of camp. He simply told them that they were not worthy of hunting in Wyoming because they did not show consideration for nature. Needless to say, they were bewildered and furious, mainly because without a guide they couldn't hunt any longer. (Out of state hunters were required to be accompanied by a licensed guide). I don't believe they really understood that their actions were unbefitting a hunter. But I learned that there is so much more to hunting than "getting game." It doesn't matter if your goal is a trophy rack or meat for your family for the year. What is most important is how one respects nature. The departure of that group of hunters left a void in the schedule until the next group arrived. That week was the best of all in camp that season. Grant and I rode horses, rebuilt the corral, and spent lot of time talking and laughing well into each evening.

Everything about camp in the Gros Vente was beautiful. Each night there was a cow moose and her calf that would appear on a ridge above camp. The sight was stunning as the sunset broadcast their silhouettes. There was a beaver down the road that worked full time cutting down trees to get his dam completed before the oncoming winter. We were afraid that he was behind schedule on his dam-building project because we were too close to his pond and scaring him. It was Grant's idea that he, Leif, and I would cut down some trees then push the logs out to him in the water. That beaver truly seemed to appreciate our help. There was a cowboy and a herd of cattle from their high country grazing area that slowly made their way through our camp on their way to the ranch below. At any point we could walk out our tents and noisily be greeted by bellowing cattle walking by. Early mornings I would rise before dawn, along with Grant and his guide (Leif Lie) and wrangler, to break the ice on the pond in order to draw fresh water for coffee. It actually wasn't as glamorous as it sounds. The real reward was being part of the camp team and, as the only woman, an equal and respected member. As our leader, Grant encouraged such an environment.

I don't want to imply that Grant was perfect, however. There were certainly some questionable habits that he demonstrated. One was the way that he lit the fire in the wood stoves in our canvas tents. He instructed me to fill the galvanized steel stove with wood, douse it with kerosene and then toss a match clear across the room into the stove. Poof! Effective, but hardly safe. Grant and I both smoked in those days and when his ashtray in the truck was full he would open the door and empty it right out on the ground. I used to lecture him about littering, warning that his ranch would soon have a floor of butts extending over the entire 2,400 acres. Surprisingly, he stopped this behavior, at least in front of me. Grant loved to joke and rib as well. One evening, questioning the wranglers about chewing tobacco, Grant suggested I try it. Feeling the peer pressure, I did, only I swallowed the juice. Needless to say, they all made their own dinner that night as I was indisposed!

Grant was a good sport and generally easy going. He just loved all the wildlife! He never had a bad word to say about my cooking. At the end of the season, he gently informed that I was the first cook in history to receive no (monetary) tips from the hunters! He didn't even get mad at me when all his clothes were stolen from the laundromat. I'd sent for a friend to lunch with during a trip to town and had stepped away from the laundry for a brief period.

It had really pained Grant to lead an old horse or mule up into the hills and shoot it for "bear bait" for hunters. I know he was secretly thrilled when Grandpa, an ancient mule, escaped the night before his scheduled execution on Sheep Mountain. Boy, did he laugh! He also accused me of being in on the caper by opening the gate… Too bad they found ol' Grandpa though!

AFTER NOTE:

Maureen F. Curley is the Executive Director of the Massachusetts Service Alliance, a nonprofit agency that is designated as the state commission on service and volunteerism. She has over 20 years of experience in the nonprofit field. Maureen is typical of the type of people Grant has hired, or lured, to help him at his ranch and many of whom Grant has stayed in touch with through the years. He remembers with as much enthusiasm and detail the people he has shared camp coffee with as any of his horses. Maureen, like me, and an untold amount of other fellow Two Bar Ranch staffers never hide the fact of Grant's influence on us. It remains a common bond. In some small way Grant made each of us better. He provided us with a glimpse and the experience of western life that would ultimately give us a deeper appreciation of our own. Grant helped get us fit for what was to come in our futures, just like he readies his young horses for what is expected from them in their ranch lives. In the course of my conversations with Maureen she called Grant and Abie and booked a summer pack trip in August of 2003 for her and her husband. I can't wait for her to share with me those stories!

Chapter Thirty-Four

MEET ME ON THE GREEN!

Grant Beck, as much as any man alive in this century, can appreciate the incredible rigors confronted by the frontiersman of Wyoming's lore. For over 60 years, Grant has lived, wrangled, cowboyed, and guided in the same country and terrain where the mountain men of yesteryear became legendary, a time when warding off hostile Indians or ferocious grizzly bears while trapping beaver and other fur-bearing critters was the daily fare. And for 16 years, from 1825 to 1840, those trappers and explorers could look forward to an annual gathering to share their tales and celebrate their lives. This occasion of merriment, mercantile, and audacious behavior was labeled a "rendezvous," and was the highlight of the mountain man's year. And, if for no other reason, surviving another season in Wyoming's harsh wilderness, was reason enough to attend this buckskin bash.

"Rendezvous" is a French word meaning "appointed meeting place." It was a time when the trappers, Indians, and fur companies convened at some pre-determined destination in the Wyoming wilderness to sell their furs, trade or barter for supplies, and exchange stories with old and new friends who had chosen the same mountain-man way of life. As you would expect at an event where the whiskey flowed freely, the behavior of the attendees was cause for alarm especially for first-time participants. For weeks on end, up to 500 mountain men and as many as 3,000 Indians gathered at the rendezvous site where they were pitted against one another in any and every type of contest including gun duels, marksmanship, horse racing, gambling, storytelling, wrestling and anything else imaginable. The one thing that was constant during all of these competitions was the absence of sobriety. One can hardly conjure up an image of these early mountain west happenings. They were clearly not for the faint of heart.

William Ashley of the American Fur Company is credited with the innovation of the Rendezvous. He was looking for the most efficient way to collect the thousands of pelts that had been garnered during a full year of trapping. In addition there was no simple means by which to replenish the supplies that were needed by the trappers to survive the extreme conditions of the Rocky Mountains and continue their trade. A summer meeting was ideal because the animals whose pelts were in demand were only trapped at the time they adorned their thick winter coats – when they would bring top dollar. A central meeting place would solve all of the problems and provide the perfect setting for what was surely the first "woodsie" of this magnitude.

Of the 16 Rendezvous that were held during the height of the Rocky Mountain fur trade, six of those were located in the Green River Valley, approximately eight miles west of what is today the town of Pinedale, WY, and coincidentally, the home of Grant Beck. The first Green River Rendezvous, held in 1833, took place near what is today the town of Daniel, WY. And the cry, "meet me on the Green" became the invitational cant that spread through the Rocky Mountain wilderness signifying that Rendezvous and the five that were to follow hosted in the Green River Valley as well as to serve notice to all prospective attendees.

To ensure these historical events were never forgotten, the folks of Sublette County created a pageant to re-tell and re-live what they consider to be the foundation of their communities. In 1936 the first Green River Rendezvous Pageant was held by the town of Daniel, near the original Rendezvous location on Horse Creek at its confluence with the Green River, to re-enact those events of the early 1800s that can be credited with opening up the American West to trade and settlement. The area residents were cast in the roles of the legends from their mountain-man past including Jim Bridger, Joe Meeks, Jedidiah Smith, John C. Fremont, Kit Carson, Joe Walker and others.

Grant Beck on Aerial (left) acting out the role of Sir William Drummond Stewart.

The Pageant's growth in popularity, and need for a more spectator-friendly site, initiated its relocation in 1960 to an area behind the Pinedale Rodeo Grounds where it is still held today the second week of July. But it was 1940 – Grant Beck was 14-years-old when he participated in his first Rendezvous. He was working at the Richardson Place near Daniel when July rolled around and time came for the annual re-enactment. Like most of the area residents, Grant did not pass on the chance to participate. As was the case with most his age, his first role was probably as an Indian brave and would have provided him the opportunity to whoop and holler while riding around bareback during the Pageant displaying his early horsemanship. But the role Grant eventually fell into after the Rendezvous moved to Pinedale, having participated the past 20 years in Daniel, was that of Sir William Drummond Stewart. Grant was cast in the role of this colorful Scotsman for almost 40 years making his participation in the Rendezvous one of the most tenured of any Sublette County resident – almost 60 years. Grant, like most everything else he did, brought both passion and flair to his role donning colorful tartan trousers and always riding one of his fancy well-groomed horses. It was the case of colorful playing colorful.

William Drummond Stewart was a wealthy Scottish nobleman. He was a veteran of the Battle of Waterloo, who, following the disbandment of his regiment, had an insatiable yearning for adventure. Ten years of his life were spent in the Rocky Mountains as a pioneer and fur trader. Unlike most of his counterparts, he had no interest in the fur trade for money; his motivation was purely for the sport of hunting all of North America's wild game animals. Sir William participated in five consecutive Rendezvous, from 1833 through 1837, and was renowned for always bringing the finest accoutrements to the annual event requiring as many as three wagons, 19 carts and as many as 50 men to transport. He regularly put up what was considered then to be obscene amounts of money for horse racing events. At one Rendezvous, Stewart even carted in a full suit of armor in which Jim Bridger was later seen stumbling around while nursing a drunken stupor.

The author's daughter donning Indian garb around 1991.

Over the 60 years of Grant's involvement, he has supported the Green River Rendezvous Pageant in a number of roles. For years he was head of the teams and wagons of which there were always dozens. He has always supplied a number of horses to the annual event. Probably, most memorable, for the hundreds of kids Grant hosted at his annual Two Bar Spear summer camp, they each got to don Indian garb and participate. My daughter, Heather, has very fond memories of being fitted for a buckskin dress, a black braided wig, and having a skin darkening cream applied to all of her bared skin to bring authenticity to her role. What a wonderful experience and memory to compliment the horse riding, camping and fishing Grant annually supplied to the mostly city-raised youth.

There was a year or two in the course of his involvement that Grant found himself in more traditional mountain man garb in the role of Joe Walker instead of the frivolous Scotsman Stewart. Joseph Reddeford Walker was a bourgeois – a supervisor of other trappers – and member of the Bonneville and Fremont Expeditions. When the bottom fell out of fur-trading, due to the fashion swing away from the traditional style of hats made from beaver pelts, Walker later found himself sheriff of Independence, MO.

By the 1840s the beaver hat was no longer all the rage with the whim of fashion turning to the new silk hat as the preference for dandies. Although an era had passed, and gone was the need for a Rendezvous, this epoch in our country's history had a more significant contribution to life in the West – it had opened the doors to western expansion and settlement thereby providing a home to the future heroes of the West – cowboys and ranchers like Grant Beck.

I will never forget my first Rendezvous. The re-enactment was movie quality. I was enamored by the pomp and procession. But nothing could compare to the party afterwards. The entire town of Pinedale turned into one great big open bar room. It was visions of new and old all mixed together: county residents socializing and partying in their authentic Rendezvous garb; local cowboys in from the area ranches to partake in the festivity with a mind to tying-one-on; and the tourists and shutterbugs who couldn't seem to get enough of it all, both pointing-at and particpating-in the spectacle. By early evening, I found myself in the back room of the Cowboy Bar, sitting amongst a table of total strangers, drinking anything and everything bought for me – rarely having to fend for myself. I was getting an eyeful from a couple of mountain men – Charlie Golden and his son Charlie, Jr., who were sitting in the center of the crowd, having lost some wager, having their scalps and faces totally shaved. They must have spent years growing their hair and beards to authenticate their roles. They probably couldn't even remember the reason for their loss. It was almost surreal, but probably the closest happening resembling Rendezvous of the past that had occurred that day. It was amidst this chaos that Grant Beck found me and asked me if I'd help him during that fall's hunting season as a guide and wrangler.

It was the summer of 1976. The Rendezvous party was even more celebratory that year in lieu of our nation's 200th anniversary. I had met Grant early that spring when I purchased my first horse from him. Whether Grant had sought me out, or it was mere chance, I still don't know to this day. I vaguely remember saying that I'd move my things out to the ranch the next day. As with the Rendezvous of old, this one had provided the perfect setting for meeting new friends, along with the traditional pageantry, story telling and merriment. Fortunately for me, I had not tipped too many to not take my new-found friend up on his offer.

The next few months for me, guiding hunters and wrangling horses, in the Jim Bridger Wilderness, were as close as one could come today in experiencing the most remote flavor of the life of the mountain men of this area's past. To experience the mountain wilderness of the Tetons and the Wind River Range with Grant, I'm sure was akin to traipsing through the wilderness along with mountain man Joe Meek. Like Grant, Meek was a renown storyteller. One of his best is Meek's telling of four trappers playing cards with the body of a dead comrade serving as the card table.

I wonder if Meek's tales were accompanied by the serving of some camp coffee – black, grounds-enhanced coffee spiked with a shot of Rendezvous whiskey?

Grant Beck on Yeller playing Joe Meeks at the Green River Rendezvous in Pinedale, July 1998.

An almost-broke Bud and me standing next to "my" fence along the East Fork River in 1976.

Chapter Thirty-Five

BUD

"You was pretty much all broke-in when you come to work for me"
Grant Beck recalled hiring me the summer of 1976

The term "green" is used to describe a level of experience or, more specifically, a level of inexperience. It is used often in the West referring to both young, unbroken horses and the rawness in a young ranch hand. That moniker was especially befitting of me and the first horse I purchased in the spring of 1976.

There is little opportunity to hire on as a ranch hand in February for a Wyoming outfit. The winter of '76 found me doing light construction work in Kemmerer, WY, for a start-up construction company owned by Larry Vance. Larry had been referred to me by Mark Stockton, a banker in Dubois. Mark and Larry had been partners along with Rusty Gouch in the Triangle R. They were licensed outfitters based out of Pinedale, WY. Rusty had earned some notoriety around the area for doing cigarette commercials. Mark had earned a reputation as being one of the best Bighorn sheep hunters in those parts. And Larry, who I liked but felt I never really got to know, had married Libby Stone, the daughter of a Pinedale rancher. Harv Stone was respected by everyone that knew him and reknown as being one of northwest Wyoming's best cowboys. Like Grant he was a seasoned veteran – but maybe just a bit more seasoned relative to his being senior to Grant in age. Harv's life, I'm sure, is every bit as colorful as Grant's. Hopefully someone, someday, will share it with the rest of us.

John Roup also worked that winter for Western Wyoming Construction Company. We met while working as laborers for Larry's company. John had ten acres along the East Fork River in Boulder, WY. Boulder was about 11 miles south of Pinedale. John, like me, was trying to eek out a living while his wife and two daughters were watching over the home place. During our work days together John talked of getting an outfitter's license that spring and starting a guiding business of his own. John was a transplant from Indiana: a cowboy-guide-outfitter wanna-be. And although I didn't know it initially, he knew less about horses and hunting than I did. He did teach me to fly fish. As I remember, he was a fairly accomplished fisherman. The first fish I caught with my new-found skill was a two-and-a-half pound German brown trout out of the East Fork River about 40 feet from the horse barn I called home.

If I had desired to do grunt work I could've gotten a construction job anywhere in the U.S., and certainly somewhere in a more moderate climate than Wyoming. So, as soon as there was a hint of spring and warmer weather, I found myself signing on to Roup's new venture. It was not at all what I had envisioned and certainly void of the least bit of glamour. My living quarters were provided by clearing out the tack room of his log-constructed horse barn. There were no utilities. Not only was it damp and cold but it leaked when it rained. I built a bed frame out of logs and scrap lumber to, at the very least, elevate my sleeping bag off of the damp, dirt floor. Thank God for Northface. I had purchased a new goose down sleeping bag before I left Kansas City that was rated at 50 below zero. I didn't freeze at night but it did take some motivation to crawl out of my mummy-style bag on frigid spring mornings.

Thus was the beginning of my career as a wrangler, guide, ranchhand – a cowboy. There was one thing missing. I didn't have a horse. Since Roup couldn't afford to pay me – I was working for room and board – I found some odd jobs in town to get enough money together to buy my first horse. After a couple weeks of putting a cedar shake roof on an A-frame home in Pinedale, I found myself flush enough with money to start looking for my steed – a necessity in my new chosen career.

Through all of the things I had encountered at that point in my young life, I had acquired a fair amount of common sense. That trait, along with a bit of luck, served me well when selecting a rancher to buy a horse from. Grant Beck's Two Bar Spear Ranch had been referred to me by more than one person in Pinedale. And when I met him that May, I instantly knew two things: a far as cowboys and horsemen went, he was the real deal and, Grant was honest.

In the pasture to the north of the drive into Grant's ranch there was a group of about 20, three-to-four-year-old horses. Some barely started and all fairly green. Having nothing else to go by, I simply chose the one that caught my eye. Grant told me his name was Bud. He was a three-year gelding and had been started but was only green-broke. I pretended to know what he was taking about and confirmed my decision. Grant won't sell a horse that he doesn't at least offer to saddle-up and have you ride. I, of course, was game. Grant's big leopard Appaloosa stud horse – Chip – was already saddled. He rounded up the young herd into his sorting corral. Grant sorted through them, letting them back out to the pasture one-by-one until Bud was left alone. Minutes later he had led Bud into the barn, saddled and bridled him, and had him snubbed up to the big stud. This entire exercise was new to me and I recorded every detail to memory.

Snubbing a horse involves taking the lead rope that is connected to the halter of an unbroken or green horse like Bud, and tying it to the saddle horn of a well-trained and broke horse like Chip. That enables the rider of the mature horse to control the movement of the "wild" one. Had I known anything about what I was witnessing I would have immediately realized I was purchasing more horse than I knew how to handle.

I climbed aboard Bud on Grant's cue and he led me around the breaking corral – a pen just big enough for a couple of horses to maneuver in. There was no way Bud could buck or act up under the circumstances. I could sense that the horse was anxious, but not nearly as much as I was. I acted satisfied with my choice but was mostly too proud and scared to admit otherwise. Of course, my only experience with riding horses to that point was on stable horses once in Southeast Missouri and during a couple of family vacations to Colorado. But I truly liked this gelding. Sometimes you can just look at a horse and you like it. We loaded him up in a borrowed horse trailer and I handed Grant a check for $350, shook his hand and thanked him. Leaving the ranch it occurred to me that the Two Bar Spear was the type of place I had envisioned working for when I left Kansas City for Wyoming that February. I said nothing to John Roup.

Now I had a horse but no saddle. First thing I did was change his name to Sundance after Robert Redford's character portrayal of Butch Cassidy's sidekick. Roup had an old saddle and bridle that I borrowed until I bought my own. Although I had never broke a horse, let alone trained one, how hard could it be? To this day, looking back, it is a minor miracle that I didn't end up hospitalized. A pattern formed after the first couple of days that lasted literally for weeks. The highlight after the first day of trying to ride this horse was Roup getting thrown head first into one of the corral posts and knocked-out cold. He was going to teach both me and the horse a thing or two. As soon as he climbed aboard, Roup started jerking Sundance's mouth and handling him rough. This, of course, followed several attempts by me to get on and stay on for more than a few seconds. Roup's character revealed itself to me after that first day when he pledged to want no more of that horse. He wished me luck. So it was up to me and, of course, Sundance. It became immediately clear to me that Roup knew nothing about horses. And as green as that horse might have been, I'm pretty sure I was greener.

People have often asked me why I didn't go buy an older well-broke gelding gentle enough for a child. The best answer is that I wanted to be a real cowboy. I figured enduring the process of this horse and I learning together would be one of the most valued lessons I could ever have. I was right. After the better part of three weeks, with an untold number of bruises and contusions, Sundance and I came to an understanding. Actually it was a form of mutual respect – a kinship. We grew to know each other. The horse teaching me about him and his learning about me (although Sundance taught me a hell of a lot more than I did him). He quickly became the best, most dependable horse of the five head on Roup's place – hands down.

The next time Grant saw me, I had quit Roup and moved to an apartment in town. I had helped Roup set up his business, had by myself fenced in his ten acres with pine poles and posts I had harvested from the forest and hauled down the mountain with a forest permit. I had wrangled, cooked and cared for the five dudes and seven horses we took on our first pack trip through the Bridger Wilderness of the Wind River Range. The clincher for me was after that first pack trip when Roup traded for new furniture for his house in lieu of cash payment for the trip. After three months of the hardest work of my life I had still not been compensated one red cent and was living in quarters where I would almost have to bathe in insect repellent nightly to be kept from being carried away by that season's onslaught of mosquitoes.

Grant had seen me that June afternoon. I hadn't seen him. Sundance was being boarded in a pasture just outside of town with some other horses. I went out daily to see him and rode when my work schedule permitted. I was working odd jobs doing whatever I could to earn a paycheck. That particular day Grant watched my pre-ride ritual. There was no corral or means of wrangling a horse easily in the pasture. I would pull up to the top of the field with my tack stuffed in the trunk of my car, along with a feed bucket and sack of sweet feed. Grabbing my halter, lead rope, and bucket of grain, I would climb through the fence and walk generally a quarter of a mile to where the horses were. Sundance would come to me as soon I was close enough that he could sense the feed. As he nibbled on the grain, I would slip the halter over his head, loop the lead rope over his neck and fasten it to the far side of the halter – thereby creating a make-shift head stall and reins. With the bucket in my left hand grasping the looped lead rope, I hopped up on his bare back and rode him back up to the car where I could tie him up to groom and saddle him. It wasn't until years later that Grant told me what had so impressed him about my command of the young horse that I had bought from him and, furthermore, what had stirred his interest in hiring me.

Bud and I at Summit Lake on my first pack trip as a wrangler in 1976.

"I had a girl helping me that spring ride these (young horses). Had a lot of colts (then), worse than now. She rode bareback horses in the rodeo, and was winnin'. She had rode Bud about ten or twelve times. I couldn't see any gain in him. I had cattle on the ranch and would

be breakin' work horses pitchin' this away with both sides of my hands. I got some pretty good work horses out of it. Anyway, I was watchin' her work Bud. When I'd seen he hadn't gained anything since the last week, I said,

'Let me ride him a little bit.'

Her mother was there – this girl's mother. I got on him and rode him around alright. He wasn't respondin' hardly any when I was tryin' to get him to go a little quicker. So I bust him on the hind end with the bridle reins and he blew up. He bucked me off and knocked me out colder than hell. The girl come in the arena. I had a small arena, and they come in there, her and her mother. When I come to and looked up at the mother, she had my head in her lap, and her daughter was cryin'.

The girl's name was Mary Jane, and her mother was American Indian. She looked Indian, too. They had an outfit on the Salmon River (Idaho). Mary Ann was a pretty damn good horseman. She must have started ten or 15 (colts) for me. But she wasn't very dependable. I think I was givin' her five dollars a head, and she'd make $15 to $20 a day. Then she'd go spend it on beer. She was 18 years old. It was only about a mile and a half to town and she'd go down to the store or bar and buy beer.

She had her own apartment in town, a little dinky place. I went in there one morning, when I was done feedin', to see what the problem was (with her not showing up). Christ, I could hardly get in there for the beer cans.

I traded around and got a really good barrel racing horse. Mary Jane really wanted it. I said all right, and told her I'd give her that horse if she'd ride these four head for a month. Well, I give her that horse after 25 days. Every colt she'd started for me, except Bud, had turned out great. All four of them were out of my Triple Chick stud, including the one you got (Bud). That girl went on in the barrel racing world after I'd given her a signed transfer on that horse, and won the state of Idaho in barrel racing."

Of the hundreds of horses Grant has broke and started, none had thrown him harder or broke him up worse than Bud. Upon hearing that, of course, I felt all the better about my accomplishment. Grant had cracked a few ribs, was bedridden for a week, and not back in the saddle for almost a month. Sundance (Bud) had turned out to be one helluva horse. I sold him the next year to a rancher. Grant followed that horse's career, as he does with all the horses he's raised when he's able to. Bud became the lead horse for that outfit. I guess Grant was proud of the both of us.

Over the years, Grant Beck and the author have often reminisced about earlier days.

Chapter Thirty-Six

THANKS FOR THE MEMORY

Courtesy of Peter T. Tomaras

In August of 1977, I booked my daughter and me on a trail ride with Grant Beck into the Wind Rivers. Natalie was 13 and liked horses. Having hunted Elk with Glidden McNeel out of Jackson some years before, I loved the mountains and the big country. I thought we'd enjoy it greatly and somehow settled on Grant as an outfitter.

The other day I saw a copy of *American Cowboy* lying on a table at Parkland College where I teach. A friend of mine writes cowboy poetry and had mentioned this magazine. Something told me to pick up the magazine – there might be something in there that interested me. I can't tell you how excited I got (at age 65) to see Grant's face looking at me from page 42, and to see Grant cinching up a horse on page 44. Grant mounted us well and gave us a hell of a nice ride back then. I'm pleased to see he's been at it ever since. Grant has been a big influence on thousands of young lives, especially those of young girls, who seem to be more into horses than boys.

Of course, Grant wouldn't remember our names out of the thousands, let alone what we might have looked like. If I remind him of some of the facts I wrote down, he might remember something about that trip. First of all, my correspondences in February and May of '77 were with Kathryne (Kyle). (Kathryne was not Grant's wife.) I see there's a different Mrs. Beck nowadays; none of my concern.

Grant drove us from the ranch back to the Log Court Motel. Later he picked us up and took us to dinner at the VFW. Don't know why we got special treatment? I clearly remember the VFW. As we entered, to the right was the bar, to the left the dining room. The three of us took a table in the dining room. Grant and I chatted about hunting and outfitting and land values after we ordered. I saw him looking over my shoulder into the bar quite a bit.

Marshall Pearson fishing at Little Trapper, ca. 1985.

"Would you care for a drink?" he asked. His eyes shifted to mine as if to read how I felt about it, what with my young daughter there.

"Would you take one?" he queried.

"Sure," I replied.

Grant bounded out of his chair and led the way to the bar, where he knew just about everyone. Eventually our food was served and we went back to the table and ate. The next morning Grant picked us up at 6:30. We had breakfast in town and afterwards drove up to the packing corral. We packed eight mules. A wrangler led the pack string, followed by the dudes. One mule ran loose (not tied to the rest of the string) and we had the extra horses.

It was a good ride to our first camp at 8,200 feet, only about eight miles into the wilderness. We hobbled the horses and had just got the tents pitched when a shower hit. We had lunch then sacked out until four or so. At 6:00 p.m. came a heavy hailstorm, followed by cold rain and wind. We provided shelter to a backpacker from Omaha. There was hail in the creamed corn and mashed potatoes when dinner got served at 6:30. Following supper we did some fishing at Little Trapper, came back by nine and roasted marshmallows. Natalie and I were up at 6:00 the next morning, started the fire and put on the coffee. The wrangler rode out to gather horses that had scattered quite a bit. Natalie and I took a short walk and saw a cow moose with her calf.

After breakfast we left camp, passed Big Trapper, Neal, Gottfried, on to Borum Lake at 9,000 feet. Natalie caught the first cutthroat and brook trout, the largest running about ten inches. We saw a squall coming, got into slickers just in time and waited it out. When it blew through we hit the trail, getting back to camp about 4:15 to find two tents down. We cleaned the fish, put them on (the fire) along with a lamb casserole (so say my notes!).

Next day we moved to the second camp at Summit Lake, at 10,300 feet. Arrived at noon, munched a picnic lunch, then set up camp. Natalie and I chose our tent site. We got the tent up just before it began to rain. We crawled inside and waited out one hell of a fierce storm: heavy rain, then snow. The temperature plummeted. Two tents went down. Those occupants and their gear got wet. After three hours the storm passed. It was about 5:00 p.m. Ice clung to the tent walls. We got the fire started and had a steak dinner by 6:45. After dinner we were all too tired and it was too cold for us to fish. But Grant and the boys caught some good trout. We sat around the campfire until 9:30 and then climbed into the tent for a COLD night!

I had a down bag and was none too warm; Natalie's was a cheap bag and she was cold. I should have taken her into my bag with me, but she had just turned 13...well, you know, I couldn't decide, and I let her freeze. In retrospect, that was dumb.

Natalie and I were up first again the next morning and got the fire restarted, heated water, and washed up. The others aroused, we had breakfast. Nat and I went to fish. We walked around the far side of the lake, hooked a good one but I broke her line trying to get it in. At 11:00 they shouted across the lake, calling us in. When we got into camp there was a ranger; no more fires allowed in the mountains because of severe fire hazard. We had no choice but to strike camp less than 24 hours after reaching that idyllic site and head down out of the mountains. We loaded up the mules, took off at 1:30, and were down at the corral by 5:30. It was a good ride. The youngsters loved it. I was a bit tired. That wound up our trip.

As I recall, Grant offered me money back. Can't remember now if I took the full refund, part of it, or said "no" because we did have a good couple of days and it wasn't his fault. I probably took half of it, can't really remember. But I do remember that Grant had the integrity to offer money back. I've got my notes, the letters from Kathryn, and the camp brochure ($265 combination trip for 7 days; $132.50 for children under 12). Also, I have a signed copy of *Wind River Trails* by Finis Mitchell, which Grant probably gave to us, and some forest maps.

Grant did things right then and has been doing them right ever since. He's a good man. He mounts the dudes well and enriches their lives. I wondered then where he got the patience to deal with the giggly little girls and us other dudes, but obviously there was something about the whole thing that he found rewarding. As a teacher these past 18 years, maybe I can relate.

Grant Beck leading a long pack string high above timberline near the Elbow Creek drainage in the Wind River Range, August 1964.

Chapter Thirty-Seven

MAX OVERBOARD:

A TWO BAR SPEAR PACK TRIP

Courtesy of Lee Gilbert

AUTHOR'S NOTE: No Two Bar Spear Ranch pack trips were ever the same and they all are memorable. Each person who has participated on one of Grant's trips through the years holds different events or experiences near to their hearts. As difficult as it is to get Grant to pick his favorite horse over a span of 70 years, it is just as challenging to identify the most amazing or memorable happening from his hundreds of mountain and wilderness outings. Each of us Two Bar Spear guests has that one story that just might be the most remarkable. For Grant's first dude boy, Lee Gilbert, who made sure his children could experience the wonder of the Bridger Wilderness that he fondly remembers, this following story must surely rank as among the most representative of who Grant was, who he is, and what he is made of. It is also among the most amazing I have heard.

With my four children to be concerned about, and a few other non-related guests as well, I was duly appointed by Grant to bring up the dusty rear of the long string of horses and mules, packing out in the Wind River Mountain range with Grant and Abie. Picking up kids' hats or loose equipment that had fallen during the trek and making sure the pack string kept up with the leaders, suited me as a tail-end Charlie. Grant almost always led the string of eight pack mules with a working lead-horse, all gear – loaded packs carefully diamond hitched. In this late summer of 1987 trip, we broke camp and moved every two days, navigating a big circle around the northern part of the Wind Rivers. On camp moving days, Grant and his dogs would wrangle the stock in at day break. They would typically venture as much as a half mile from camp seeking the most nutritious grass to graze upon, even though all were hobbled. Meanwhile, Abie and her girls (summer help) would be fixing a hearty breakfast on an open cook fire. We campers would wake to the thundering hoofs and bells of the incoming horses and mules, smell the alluring chow, and roll out of our sleeping bags to splash cold mountain water upon our faces and elsewhere we deemed necessary. Once breakfast was over, we packed up our duds, took down our tents, and gathered our gear at a central location while the dishes were being done up. Pack saddles were hitched to the mules, paniards were loaded and carefully balanced for equal weight, and loading the pack mules commenced. This exercise often offered some excitement, as mules, with minds of their own, sometimes don't cotton to being packed. (I never understood why Grant, after pooh-poohing mules for all the years I knew him at the Half Moon, decided to pack out on mules at his Two Bar Spear!) With the string finally packed-up, camp and cook fires doused out, horses saddled and ready to go, we'd mount up and head out, following Grant's lead with the pack string.

On this particular lovely late morning – clear blue skies and warmed-past-frost – we'd ridden less than a couple of hours and were somewhere between Summit and Twin Lakes. Just before the trail narrowed on a long, steep, wooded embankment, Grant signaled for me to leave my rear post, and ride up to the lead where he was. He indicated he wanted me in the lead because the trail crossed a creek up ahead over a fairly high log bridge. Grant's horse was "young" and a little skittish. My horse's lead would settle him down.

The trail to the creek bridge was narrow, and made a sharp 90-degree right turn up onto a log bridge about 100 feet long, then a sharp 90-degree left turn off the bridge. The trail immediately entered a group of switch-backs going up a steep hill on the other side. The bridge wasn't so high that it needed more than a large log lying long-ways as a guardrail on each edge of the bridge. The water rushing under the bridge was a raging torrent of glacial fed, icy water coming off the mountain in a boulder strewn channel. I'd ridden across this bridge many times before. While I wasn't the little cowboy of my youth, I was confident in my ability to ride across, and proud in the confidence Grant was showing in me to lead. Up and over the bridge I rode, sensitive to Grant and his young horse following me. I turned left off the structure and immediately broke onto the trail. I had a great view back of the rest of the string coming across. The sun was bright. Grant on his

Grant Beck on Buckshot leading Max.

young horse was doing just fine. Grant held the lead rope to Max – the packed, lead workhorse next in line. The eight mules following Max were tied first to him and then one another on down the line. Just as the draft horse-bred Max clumped onto the bridge, the mule immediately behind and tied to him cut the corner onto the bridge, fetching up against the corner of the bridge. The butt-end of the log guard rail caused the first mule to rare back. Max, in mid-stride onto the bridge, was pulled off balance. To our amazed-horror, the huge horse toppled over sideways. Max plunged downward, 12 feet or so, on his back – pack first – out of my sight, into the boulder-strewn torrent of white, freezing water. Grant, who'd let go his lead rope to Max, dismounted mid-bridge, hollered at me to grab his horse, and without hesitation jumped off the bridge into the frigid rapids after Max.

I was stunned. How quickly this beautiful, bright sunny day had turned into mayhem. Maybe my eyes had deceived me. I tried to fast-rewind to the instant of disaster, back to the serenity before, and away from the horror transpiring before me. I leaped off my horse. I tied him to a bush blocking the trail. I edged past Grant's horse, which seemed particularly undisturbed standing alone on the bridge amidst this disaster, and peered over the side. The prospects were alarming – not only were we going to lose a good horse, but Grant was being tossed around like a bobble in crippling 30-something degree water, to what end? Max somehow miraculously righted himself in the water. He found some footing, and in the big horse's struggle to climb out, had wedged a hoof between two enormous boulders by the side of the creek. Grant was fighting to get upstream to Max's head to hold him still, calm him and then guide him out. A young ranch hand on the trip, who had been following just behind Grant's pack train, dismounted and joined me on the bridge. The rest of the riders were just a short distance away.

I hollered at Grant that Max had a leg wedged in the rocks and that it might be broken, as it was turned at a bad angle. Grant and Max, the horse almost reading Grant's mind, carefully worked the leg out, and somehow he got Max backed out from between the large boulders at the water's edge, still belly-deep in water. Grant hollered up for us to get a remarkably calm Max unpacked. I found I could straddle the water with one foot on a boulder and the other foot on Max's back, and motioned our wrangler to get on the other side and do the same. We untied the diamond hitch from on top, and started heaving off tents, soft packs, and finally the paniards up onto the bank. With the situation more or less under control and Max resting calmly, a huge commotion flared- up back on the trail by the entrance to the bridge.

The mules had been milling around this short while, which is not a good thing for mules who are packed and tied together. Abdul – mule carrying the kitchen pack with the eggs – had gotten the lead rope to the next mule behind caught between his rear legs. This irritation had caused him to start kicking, trying to clear the rope. As Abdul kicked, the mule tied behind was trying to get out of the way which tightened the rope between them causing more irritation between Abdul's legs. The more Abdul kicked, the more the lead rope dug into his hide. Abdul soon started launching both feet about as fast as a series of prize-fighter jabs. Meanwhile, unpacking Max lightened his load enough to provide Grant the chance of getting him safely out of the water and up the steep embankment. The three of us were left helpless to do anything about Abdul.

You can imagine how the rest of the mules were reacting to the commotion. The more Abdul kicked, the more the next mule was maneuvering to get out of the way which balled up all the rest of the string which was tied together by lead ropes. Just when we had Max settled down and the pending disaster under control, Abdul starts going nuts. The lead mule had created enough ruckus with the rest of the string to a point where one of those damned mules might really get hurt. This situation completely redefined "hell and high water" for me!

Well, first things first. The wrangler and I got Max unloaded in record time. Nobody had lost their heads except Abdul. Grant, hypothermia shock now wearing off, somehow turned the now unloaded Max around, and led him up and over the boulders out of the angry creek. Max's leg seemed uninjured and he only had a few abrasions to show for his high-diving stunt. By now, Abdul had kicked himself into complete exhaustion, and had collapsed on the ground, broken-egg-gruel leaking out of his pack, down onto his neck, and up towards his head. Grant, as the urgency of the moment was wearing off and in a rage over Abdul, who had seemingly taken advantage of Grant's inability to attend to his lead rope problem, stormed over to the prone mule. He started blistering him with low growling epithets as he kicked him up onto his feet. About that time, the rest of the riders had caught up with us at the bridge, saw Grant kicking a mule down on the ground, and thought the egg gruel was Abdul's brains leaking out of his head. It certainly is hard to make sense out of situations when all you have to go by is at the tail end.

In the end, we repacked Max, repacked Abdul – now too tired and/or too scared to complain – remounted our horses, which had just been a quiet and appreciative audience, and completed the crossing.

I'll never forget the calmness with which Max took his plunge and then re-entered the game. I'll never forget Grant's spontaneously wild jump off the side of the bridge down into the treacherous, icy cold water. When I hear someone say to me that "so and so" would take the shirt off their backs for "so and so," all I can think of is Grant risking his life and limb, without hesitation, to go after a horse I'd all but written off, on a bridge way up in the Wind Rivers, a 1,000 miles from home.

Chapter Thirty-Eight

OOPS,

I CAUGHT AN EAR

Many of Grant's relationships are cross-generational.
All of them are special.

It is no different with my family. I first worked for Grant Beck in 1976. It's an easy year to remember because it was our nation's 200th-year anniversary. In 1988 my youngest daughter, Heather, spent her first year at the Two Bar Spear Ranch's kid camp. Her mother, my wife, Sally, was understandably a little anxious about sending her eight-year-old daughter 600 miles from home to a seemingly remote ranch in northwest Wyoming for three weeks. Beyond trusting my opinion, Sally had met Grant. She had had her first horseback ride on an early fall day in 1980 on an old Appaloosa horse named Saul (Saul had the distinction of being blind in one eye). She had spent a beautiful sunny afternoon high in the Teton National Forest napping adjacent to Grant in the soft mountain grass on a hillside overlooking Slide Lake. I believe they both had their hats pulled over their eyes.

Heather journeyed to Pinedale. Grant's camp was still coed at that time; now it is for young female campers only. Grant was always partial to the girls. At a young age they typically took so much better to the horses than boys. Wes Miller wrote the following story after he attended that same camp. Wes, too, was eight-years-old. Today Wes is an accomplished horseman and rodeo performer. The Miller Ranch is one of the most renown in northwest Wyoming. In fact, in his younger days, Grant had actually worked for Wes' grandfather, Bob Miller. This is Wes' version of the story as he wrote it for his third grade English class at school.

Once when I was a little boy I went on a pack trip in the mountains above Pinedale. The leader of the group was Grant Beck. He was a nice old man and one heck of a pack trip leader. Our destination was Trapper Lake and it was about 20 miles up in the mountains. We had a

Heather Sullivan and her catch.

Wes Miller and his catch.

big string of horses and some mules to carry our luggage. The main thing we were going to be doing was fishing in Trapper Lakes. I was excited for over a month before the trip to go up there and fish. I had never been fishing in a lake so I couldn't wait to give it a try.

We left Pinedale early Saturday morning and we were going to be up there for over a week. It was toward the end of June and everything was green and beautiful. When we got to the mountains we unloaded our horses and headed up the trail to Trapper Lake. It took us at least half the day to get there and when we did I couldn't wait to get my hook in Trapper Lake. Unfortunately Grant the leader made me set up my tent instead. So I had to wait until the next morning.

When the next morning finally came I went out to Trapper Lake to go fishing. I found a big rock to stand on and sent out my first cast. I reeled it in and didn't catch a fish. After about 20 more casts I finally caught my fish. But I was disappointed cause it took me forever it seemed and I didn't catch another fish that day. So I talked to Grant that night and asked him what I could do about me only catching one fish. He told me there was a girl (Heather) on the trip with the same problem I had and that he would take me and that girl to a better lake the next morning. The next morning came early and us three headed for the good lake. On the way Grant asked me if I knew how to fish. I was scared to tell him I couldn't fish very good so I said yea of course I can fish.

It was about eight o'clock when we got to our destination and Grant put me and this girl on a big rock that kind of went out over the lake. I couldn't wait to get my hook out there. So I came from the side with my pole and sent my hook out there as far as I could. I never saw my hook enter the water and about two seconds later I heard a huge scream. I had hooked the girl right in the ear lobe. Grant had to take the girl back to Pinedale to get the hook out and I felt terrible. When Grant and the girl got back I apologized. Both of them realized I shouldn't have been a hotshot and told Grant that I didn't know how to fish so he could have taught me. That would have prevented a big accident.

– Wes Miller

Grant, Wes, and Heather got back to base camp. Wes dismounted, unsaddled and put up his horse. Grant and Heather headed down the trail and ended up completing the four-hour ride to the trailhead in the dark. Grant said Heather was a real trooper not complaining a bit the entire ride out. When they got to the vehicles, Grant trailered their two horses and drove Heather into Pinedale to the clinic to have the fishhook removed from her ear. I was in California on business when the phone rang back at our home in Bennett, CO, so Grant could inform Sally of the incident. Of course, Sally's motherly instincts were to inquire if Heather wanted to come home. Meanwhile Heather was thinking she couldn't wait to get back up to the Summit Lake camp. Things worked out for everyone, which is typical at the Two Bar Spear. The next day Grant and Heather headed back up to camp. They completed their pack trip. Grant's most distinct recollection of the entire episode was Wes asking Grant the next day,

"You think she'll still like me?"

Heather Sullivan and Wes Miller horsing around with friends and fellow campers near the campfire in high country.

Saddle bronc rider at the Pinedale Rodeo.

Chapter Thirty-Nine

A MARE FOR THE PINEDALE RODEO STRING

Grant Beck has been an outfitter in Wyoming for over 50 years. He has operated his camp for kids at the Two Bar Spear Ranch for almost as long – 46 years at the time of this writing. His most remarkable "record" in all of those years and experiences is the fact that no one has ever been seriously injured while under the responsibility of Grant or his staff; whether on horseback, on the ranch, at hunting camp, up in the Bridger Wilderness, or anywhere in between. Of course, the reason for this could be summed up in the fact that Grant cares. This is true. But more than that, Grant has uncanny good sense. The kind you can't learn from a book. I believe that it comes to him from several things. Grant was only nine when his folks died. So unlike most of us he grew up without traditional parental guidance. He learned to get along from an early age relying more than anything else on his instincts. Secondly, Grant moved away from home and his sister (who was his guardian) at the tender age of 13. He embarked upon a journey, into a Western world, where the two most important ingredients for being successful were honesty and hard work (in less than ideal conditions). These Grant learned and mastered at an age when the biggest concern for most of us is our complexion. Thirdly, Grant is innately wise. The type of wisdom one learns from doing. Not necessarily approaching things timidly, but with the idea of doing things the best one can, learning from your mistakes and misjudgments rather than repeating them. This is Grant's essence. This is why he can boast (although Grant rarely boasts) about his track record of caring and looking after people.

I never said that his campers, hunters, and dudes didn't go away with an occasional bump or bruise. One incident happened to be just a bit more severe than most; a true rarity (for Grant) in itself. In fact, to this day Grant is still embarrassed about it. And for me, even though it involved my own flesh and blood, I still cannot believe how accidents like this are almost completely void in a lifetime of experiences, adventures, and relationships such as Grant's and the Two Bar Spear.

Heather, my eldest child, started riding horses when she was about five-years-old. I was hoping to provide her something at an early age that was not readily available to me during my youth. Something that I thought would make a difference in Heather's life. To my gratification, she enjoyed it. Of course the enjoyment part of it would have not been possible, particularly for a child at that age, unless it was with the right horse. In this case it was the right horse. An Appaloosa mare that we had purchased from Grant named "Adeline." Grant believes you should never get too attached to a horse. But Adeline is one horse I'd wished I had and never parted with. She was a dandy. I'll never lose the mental image of the expression on Heather's face while competing at her first barrel racing event. It was during one of the weekly gymkhanas held in Fort Lupton, CO. Heather, in all of her glory, had urged Adeline on to a second-place finish. A father was never more proud of a five-year-old daughter. And a young lady never glowed so genuinely.

Of course soon following this feat I thought Heather was ready for summer camp at the Two Bar Spear. Grant intimated that she was still a little too young. Grant and Abie normally didn't except campers prior to the age of nine or ten. Well, we compromised a few years later and Heather was welcomed as a feisty little eight-year-old.

Fast forward to Heather's fourth year at summer camp. What I could teach her about horses and riding over 11 months of the year paled by comparison to what these young campers would learn in a few short weeks under Grant's tutelage. Heather's abilities as a horseman grew dramatically after each season. Each year it was the challenge of Grant and his staff to select the four-legged partner who would best match up with the direction each of the campers was heading in terms of skills and desire. By her fourth year, although still only 12, Heather was looking for a challenge. Like all of his stories and experiences, no one tells them better, or more heartfelt than Grant.

> *"Pretty good mare. I rode her one day here. She'd been rode about three times when I rode her. I was lopin' her all the way around the arena. We really thought we had a hell of horse. She was just comin' into three (years old), when we took her home (Pinedale). And we rode her a little bit up there. Heather always wanted a horse-a little peppier-because she was a good rider, had a lot of balance for her age. I guess it was from going to those little horse shows up there (gymkhanas in Colorado). I didn't see it happen. I was up the field irrigatin', anyway this mare blew up and bucked."*

Heather was lying on the ground before she ever knew what happened, shaken, crumpled, and stunned. Abie helped her to her feet to assess the damage: broken glasses, a bit smudged with the dirt from the corral, a tad sore, and an ego just a little bruised. It was nothing that a couple of Tylenol, a cold glass of water and a nap wouldn't fix. When Heather woke up, she was still just a little bit too sore for Grant's and Abie's liking. Assuming the role of concerned parents, they took her into Pinedale to the medical clinic. When they returned to the ranch Heather sported a rainbow cast on her right arm and quickly became the center of attention. She had a slight fracture in her right forearm. It was the result of the immediate reaction we all have when tossed from the back of one of our equine friends – reaching down with a hand to cushion the fall. Grant has always had the amazing ability to brighten the sourest turning events. Heather's mood was great. In fact, her only real disappointment came when the doctor told her he didn't want her back on a horse until her cast came off. That meant her abstaining from riding during the remainder of camp, including the pack trip. One of the best testaments I can ever pass on about Grant is this. Of course, Heather's mother and I, deeply worried, immediately offered to come and get her. Heather would have none of that. She was going to stay until the end of camp even though she couldn't ride. She'd make the best of it. Pretty impressive for a 12-year-old.

As for the mare. In Grant's words:

> *"So we never rode her again. I took her up to the Pinedale rodeo grounds. And by God last year, now this was a long time ago that we'd took her up there (nine years ago), she come out of the shoot and this guy got second place on her at the fall rodeo. She was not big. Too little for saddle bronc, but this guy was ridin saddle bronc."*

Grant Beck on his Appaloosas *(clockwise from upper left)*:
Bud, Chip, Taylor Maid with Tip trailing, and Cherokee Banjo Bill.

Chapter Forty

BUCKSHOT

It would be hard to come up with a more appropriate name for an Appaloosa horse than Buckshot. For you non-horse persons, the Appaloosa is recognized or known by its spotted coat. The pattern of the coat can vary. A leopard Appy is generally white with black or varying hues of brown spots all over. Snowflake Appys will usually be dark in color with white or light specks (flakes). An Appy that is dark in color but white on its quarters and loins with dark spots across the white area is termed – spotted blanket. While these are the primary patterns, there can be several other variations. A registered Appy can even be solid in color. But to simplify the issue, I generally refer to the traditional Appaloosa as a quarter horse with color. The most recognized Appaloosa is probably a spotted blanket Appy – Zip Cochise – that John Wayne rode in the movie *Eldorado*.

That was a handsome horse.

Grant Beck's entire herd of ranch horses on the Two Bar Spear Ranch in the era I worked for him consisted of the Quarter Horses and Appaloosas he bred and raised. Today, gone are the Appaloosas on the Two Bar Spear, replaced by a colorful herd of Paint horses that he and his wife Abie have raised.

As one might imagine, if you lived the rugged life that Grant has for some 70-odd years, you'd have had a lot of close calls. This would, I'm sure, be true for any life-long cowboy. In that type of life, while one might never really expect it, you'll find that most of those individuals seem to take those "close-calls" in stride. Things happen and then you move on.

One of Grant's many close-calls came while aboard one of his ranch-bred and ranch-raised Appaloosas. A horse he called Buckshot. This particular horse wasn't the only Buckshot reared on the Two Bar Spear. When you've raised as many horses as Grant, sooner or later you'll start to recycle names. I purchased a horse named J.B. Buckshot from Grant back in 1986. He was as pretty a horse as the one that starred in *Eldorado* – one of my all-time favorites (both horse and movie). Anyway, back to the Buckshot that stayed on the ranch:

"Abie had Jim and Jeri Davis and their three kids up at Borum Lake (one of thousands of lakes in the Wind River Mountain Range). The only people that was in camp was Kimi, Emi's sister. (Both Kimi and Emi Demotto-Riley were first campers and later counselors at Grant's ranch. Emi moved back to Pinedale after graduating from college back East.) *If it hadn't been for Kimi, it coulda ended up pretty bad. I kinda lost my wind. Buckshot had fallen with me on him, and had me pinned underneath him. Kimi grabbed a hold of my arm, braced both feet agin the horse, and just hung on. Every time Buckshot'd quiver, she'd gain a little bit. Finally, in his death throws, why, she got me out. I was pinned from mid-thigh to the top of my chest. That was about as close I ever had, I think.*

I was just gonna drag some logs in to camp. I'd had some there that wouldn't of been too hard to get cuz they was already sawed-up. Anyway, I'd got out from beneath ol' Buckshot, and then Abie returned to camp with Jim and Jeri. Jim wanted to know if I wanted to post him (Buckshot).

'Well, I don't think there is any need. He had to have had a heart attack.'

He'd start to tremble and stagger a bit, and I'd tried to get back to where I'd stacked the saddles, right in the middle of a damn mess of rocks. That's where he'd ended up fallin' with me. Then I was under him in those rocks. Fallen on the rocks is what hurt. (Grant was hurt a lot worse than he ever let on. While I don't think he broke any bones, he did have a few cracked ribs, and was bruised all over quite badly.)

'It's one of the best campsites, isn't it?' Grant asked Abie and me.

There is always feed and stuff – Clear Creek. That's a good area. We took Sam and Lucky, it took both of those horses to pull Buckshot out of camp – downhill! It's happened right in camp.

We couldn't stay at Clear Creek anymore that summer for the flies. The flies were terrible. It just wasn't because of the carcass. The horse flies that fall were God-awful. Horses during the day – we couldn't ride during the day sometimes cuz the flies were so bad. The horses were loose (hobbled) and they never left the trees. They'd never get out of those trees during the day. You could be walkin' along, swat your leg, and get a whole handful of those flies. They were terrible! Backpackers were comin' down the trail with bloody legs if they had shorts on. There was nothin' they could put on their legs to keep the flies off.

They had a ranger there (in Pinedale) that didn't know straight-up. When we got out (of the Jim Bridger wilderness) I told him I had a horse die on me.

'Be alright if I just find some timber and burn him?'

'No, we can't have no fires up there. Just drag him outta camp. Is he shod?'

'Yeah,' I says.

'Well, pull his shoes off and just drag him outta camp.'

I says, 'Go to hell. If you want those shoes off that son-of-a-bitch, why you go get 'em! (Clear Creek is about a full day's ride in on horseback, to an elevation change of about 2,000 feet to about 10,000 feet. And as banged up as Grant was, he wasn't going to be back on a horse for a while). *I never pulled the shoes off a dead horse in my life!'*

The feet are still up there with shoes on 'em. The forest service is so silly – in some ways dumb. They (someone) had a horse die up there on the trail last fall (2002). Abie, Georgia and Emi were goin' to climb Square Top. They passed this dead horse on the trail. A pretty good lookin' horse I guess. And they, nobody knew about it. They wouldn't claim it, becuz you gotta get 'em out one way or another. They won't let you burn 'em – you gotta pack 'em out. I was kinda concerned when they told me about it figurin' it would attract bears. I was worried 'bout Abie and the girls."

Dr. William Close trout fishing on the Green River not far from his Big Piney, WY, ranch.

Chapter Forty-One

ALMOST FAMOUS

For most of us, the closest we will ever get to celebrity or Hollywood, is *People Magazine*, or our local cinema. For Grant, somehow it has always found him. His brushes with celebrity, if not legendary, are certainly worth noting. Although Grant has never judged people by who they were in the public's eye, what Grant remembers about people, is just who they are as a person – their character. To Grant, rubbing shoulders with a celebrity is no more memorable or significant than having a cup of camp coffee with you or me. It has just been a part of his life.

The experiences he had during the filming of *Shane* and *Jubal* in Jackson Hole were just the beginning of it. It seems he has always been exposed to some type of celebrity throughout his life in Wyoming. Included among Grant's many friends are the Closes of Big Piney. Big Piney is a small Wyoming town about 40 miles southwest of Pinedale. Dr. Close is famous in his own right. Most Americans are more familiar with his movie actor daughter – Glenn. Grant knows Glenn, not as an award-winning actress, but as Doc Close's daughter. Grant's dealings with Glenn have merely been as one would have with the offspring of any fellow Wyoming rancher.

William T. (Bill) Close, M.D., has not just been a friend of Grant's but has also seen him as a patient. Although now retired, Dr. Close's career has been memorialized in the books he's written. While most won't draw the connection, a portion of his contributions as a physician occurred during the 16 years he spent in the Congo in Africa. This story highlights his personal involvement with one of the world's worst diseases and was revealed in the book he wrote – *Ebola: Through the Eyes of the People*.

Grant recalls when the Closes moved to Big Piney in the '60s. They purchased a ranch from the Mickelsons which was converted into a guest ranch run by their daughter, Jesse Close, Glenn's sister, and Jesse's husband, Tom. Grant praised how hard Jesse and Tom worked trying to make a go of the guest ranch.

On Dr. Close, Grant shared:

"He's getting wore out. He's a year older than I am; had eye surgery just like me. He got a disease in it, and he lost the eye. He also had a hip operation. The kids were pretty much raised when he got back from Africa. They was raised in the states by their mother, Tina. She stayed in the states mostly, so the kids got to go to boarding school. Dr. Close was Muboto's personal physician."

Grant's had numerous dealing with celebrity through his horses. Noel Skinner worked for Robert Redford's ranch in Utah. Part of that ranch was actually owned once by Grant's great grandfather.

"My granddad's ranch is what Robert Redford owns today, in Spanish Fork, UT. My Granddad Beck was one of the first landowners when they created the town. He'd had a lot of mining claims. He ended up pretty wealthy, had acquired a hell of a lot of land. He also had a hell of a large family – he was a polygamist."

Grant's family background all stems from the Mormon Church in Utah. Grant has never been active in the church and, as a result of his experiences growing up, would just as well forget that part of his history

"Dad had three half-brothers. Everyone liked my dad. But they didn't like some of Dad's full-brothers. The half-brothers were all, every one of them, good friends of my dad. They loved working with him in the mines. Their names were Mitchell, Spencer, and Brian Beck. Their mother's name was Gracie Walker. I never did know my Granddad Beck but I knew my mother didn't care for him. And I didn't like my Grandma Roundy, my mother's mother. She caused me more spankins. It was always fetch this, fetch me that. One day the newspaper was right by her rockin' chair, where she sit 40 hours a day. I was playin' with my cat, and she said,

'Fetch me that newspaper.'

I said, "Get it yourself." My mother heard me, goddamn, I got a whippin'. I just hated her for that.

Anyway, talkin' about my Grandpa Beck, he had 14 children. He died in 1929 or 1930. I

know Dad went to the funeral, and every child but Dad got $10,000 in cash – that was $130,000. Nobody wanted the farm cuz Dad was the only one who liked farming. So rather than take $10,000, Dad took machinery and work horses. He moved that stuff from Spanish Fork to Downey, ID – near Logan, ID. They moved all that stuff with horses. Dad farmed there at Downey. Mother and some of her siblings moved to Rigby, ID, including Lauren, who was the baby of Mother's family, and Grandma. Well, I know Grandma was needin' help all the time, so Dad sold in Downey and moved to Rigby with the rest of the family. That was the worst move he ever made. We fed the Roundy family – Dad did. Whenever there was a problem they'd come to us. And Grandma, there was a lot of them as helpless as she was, in my opinion. I never liked her. When she died I wouldn't go to the funeral. I stayed home and milked the cows for my sister and her husband."

Grant recalls a time or two when Noel Skinner was interested in buying a horse from him for the Redford Ranch. But I don't think any transaction ever went through. Skinner always tendered an offer that Grant seemed inappropriate, and Grant wasn't going to consummate a deal just because it involved Robert Redford, directly or indirectly.

Grant also owned at least one horse that made it to the silver screen. Grant had purchased a young two-year-old stud from a horse trader in Jackson. The horse was an albino that Grant named Whitey. The horse left Pinedale on a load of horses going to North Dakota when Grant sold him to a Pinedale horse trader. I have photos I took of Whitey from one of my many visits to The Two Bar Spear. He was in the corral near the tool shed where Grant generally kept his stud colts. He had a great disposition for a stud colt, but personally, I didn't care for his head or the color of his eyes. I remember his playing with one of the ranch kittens. It was the first time I ever saw a cat and horse playing around together. I never knew what became of Whitey until years later after I'd seen him in the movies.

"I bought him –Whitey. That's the horse that went to a horse trader named Wilson. He had the Sundance Hotel or another hotel in Pinedale. He was a lady chaser. He was supposed to have been two-years-old. I had two albino horses over the years. I got 'em out of Jackson. One was out of Cotton-eyed Joe. He was a gaited horse. But this here horse Whitey, remember his eyes were always runnin'? And he had a bad head. I got him when he come down to Pinedale

on a truckload of horses from Jackson. I ended up tradin' one or two for four or some damn thing. The horse trader always had something that was halter broke. We gelded him. Castrated him myself. But after I started to ride him, you'd touch that horse and he'd step towards you. I don't know how many times he stepped on my feet because he couldn't see."

It is not uncommon for albino horses to have vision problems.

"He was the ugliest horse I ever had. I think I had him for about two-and-half months. That's why Wilson wanted him, because he was young."

"Damn, if he didn't turn up in a movie, Dances with Wolves. *He had my brand – the Two Bar Spear brand – on him. You could see my brand on him in the movie. That's how I found out he was in it."*

Whitey was the horse that the medicine man, Kicking Bird – played by Graham Greene – rode in Kevin Costner's award-winning *Dances With Wolves*. Grant went back to see the movie several times wanting to make sure it was really his brand on that horse. I guess it goes to show you that looks aren't everything when it comes to getting into the movies.

"I went to see it twice to make sure. I didn't like the movie, it was too gory. We drove to Big Piney to see it. A neighbor was there. She said the kids sure liked it especially after they seen my brand on the horse."

Whitey when Grant owned him as a two-year-old stud colt.

Freemont Lake, Pinedale, WY.

Chapter Forty-Two

LAST DANCE

I am pretty certain that cowboys never think about their last ride. They don't refer to riding as dancing either. But after watching Grant Beck in the saddle on horseback on and off over the past 27 years, there is as much harmony between horse and rider as any Fred Astaire and Ginger Rogers duet. But this story isn't about Grant's last dance.

Ruth Jankiwiecz, a young lady from New Jersey showed up in Pinedale with her husband, Joseph, mid-summer of 2000. While the Wind River Mountain Range lakes were mostly thawed by this time, there are always some of the more than 1,000 lakes still frozen come mid-July. And in some years, there are lakes up in the Wind Rivers that never do thaw.

This couple rode into Pinedale driving a spanking new pick-up truck. Hitched to the rear of the truck was a brand new house trailer. Neither the mountain lakes in the Bridger Wilderness, nor fishing in them, are what this particular couple had in mind. Although at this time of year in Pinedale, fishing is the typical visitor activity. The Jankiwieczs' tale, though, could un-thaw the most frozen of the Wind River lakes. They stopped their rig in front of the Moose Trading Post, where Joseph went in to inquire about where a fellow might get his wife a ride on a horse. As most people who have spent anytime around Pinedale know, when it comes to horses, and when it comes to hospitality, Beck's Two Bar Spear Ranch is the safest bet.

This most sought-after ride was to be this gal's last. Her last dance if you will. What was soon to be revealed to all concerned was that this slightly built, 42-year-old woman from New Jersey, who had traveled cross–continent for a horseback ride in the West, had terminal cancer. In fact, it was this inoperable, incurable, ravaging of Ruth's physical being that had inspired Joseph to quit his job, purchase truck and trailer and head West. He not only wanted to be with her every minute until the end, but also wanted Ruth to have a chance to experience some of her life-long dreams while doing so. They were determined not to let this disease navigate their last days together.

When this 40-something couple showed up at the Two Bar Spear they were, like all strangers, immediately, warmly welcomed. Grant would have saddled-up a horse for her without any knowledge of her predicament. All Ruth was looking for was the thrill of being on a horse, something she had never experienced and, following her ride, have a photo taken of her in the saddle to be left behind as a special remembrance for Joseph. That was the type of memory Ruth and Joseph were chasing, not one of her idly wasting away in a New Jersey hospital room with Joseph standing helplessly by her side, watching and waiting.

Homer was saddled-up for Ruth. Abie Beck and sisters, Emi and Kimi Demotto-Riley, took her out for a short ride or for as long as Ruth was able to tolerate in her condition. Though her expectation was to last no more than ten minutes, Ruth was totally enraptured by the moment in spite of almost certainly experiencing some physical discomfort. The four riders returned to the corral almost an hour later where they found Grant sorting horses. Ruth's gratitude for the horse ride could not have been more expressive or sincere. But to everyone's surprise, it was another four-legged creature that captured Ruth's attention.

> *"Everyone should have the opportunity in their lifetime to own a dog like that," Ruth proclaimed.*

She was referring to one of Grant's dogs that was presently assisting in the horse sorting. You'd have to see the way that Grant's dogs have always worked for him and with him to get the gist of her meaning. That was all Ruth needed to say. After the couple left, Grant phoned the neighbor of his who raised the border collie-blue-

Ruth Jankiwiecz.

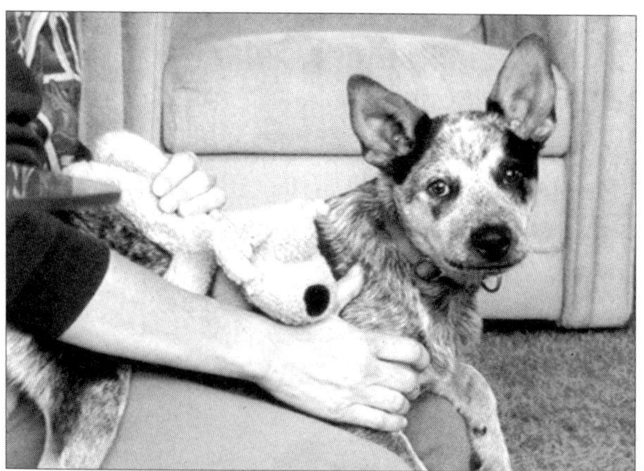

Gar.

healer-crossed pups. As luck would have it a new litter of pups were just then looking for homes.

Within a couple of days Ruth was to have a new companion. Another wish fulfilled. She ended up with the pick of the litter. And of course, no money ever exchanged hands. Ruth named the dog Gargoyle. She and Joseph called him "Gar" for short.

It was the following April before God called Ruth's number. She and Joseph, overwhelmed by their reception from the Becks and other folks in Pinedale, had rented an apartment there. One of this small, northwest Wyoming town's resident RNs checked in on Ruth three days a week. The pup never left her side. Grant saw her briefly just before Ruth passed on. He walked into her room.

"She couldn't cry," Grant proclaimed, "because she didn't have no fluid."

But Grant did cry. Ruth had had her last dance. And Grant had played a hand in picking her final partner, both of them, Homer and Gar.

Grant Beck, August 1984. *Photo courtesy of Sam Hair*

EPILOGUE

A COWBOY POET

There may be cowboys, here and gone, who've roped more calves, packed more mules, broke more colts, tossed more bales, guided more dudes and greenhorns, shoed more horses or run bigger spreads... but you'd have to search far and wide to find a cowboy who's gotten more out of life from giving to others. Grant Beck gave and is still giving. Not so much through his deeds like annually awarding one young dude kid a free "ride" at his Two Bar Spear Ranch kid's summer camp every year since he started it in 1957. And, not so much from words of cowboy wisdom such as those by Will Rogers, nor from the rhythmical expression of cowboy poets such as Baxter Black. It's the intangibles. Those things you can't measure, can't weigh, and certainly can't deposit. Grant doles out the type of learning and understanding that helps kids become adults. The kind of learning that helps adults like you and me become better adults.

Over the years Grant has provided people young and old, who have had the good fortune in spending some time with him, a natural sense of direction. Grant's demeanor and guidance, although at times brash, builds confidence and self-esteem. At the end of a day at the Two Bar Spear Ranch whether on horseback or helping Grant irrigate; or, at the culmination of a five-day pack trip in the Wind River Range, or during a week in hunting camp above the Gros Ventre, if one has been lucky enough to share a piece of Grant's life, one can't help but become a bit more self-reflective. Simple but hard, Grant's life, Grant's way, subliminally uncomplicates things. Somehow it just makes life more rewarding. Things seem to fit.

Amazingly in Grant's world, a world centered on people, the warm bodies that have assisted him most in his mission are of the four-legged variety. It wasn't Grant who coined the idea that the best thing for the inside of a person is the outside of a horse, but it certainly could have been. He has lived it. And more importantly, he has spent a lifetime helping other people live it, too. A poet suggests one who writes poems. A poem can be defined as any experience that produces an effect upon the mind, the heart, and the soul, similar or likened to that of a poem. That in mind, I maintain Grant may be remembered as one of the greatest cowboy poets of all time.

SOURCES OF PHOTOGRAPHS

VIII	Courtesy of Grant and Abie Beck Collection
P.2	Courtesy of Bob Sullivan Collection
P.3	Courtesy of Bob Sullivan Collection
1:4	Courtesy of Sam Hair Collection
1:6	Courtesy of Bob Sullivan Collection
2:7	Courtesy of Grant and Abie Beck Collection
2:8	Courtesy of Grant and Abie Beck Collection
3:9	Courtesy of Grant and Abie Beck Collection
4:12	Courtesy of Grant and Abie Beck Collection
4:15	Collection of the Jackson Hole Historical Society and Museum
5:16	Courtesy of Grant and Abie Beck Collection
5:19	Courtesy of Grant and Abie Beck Collection
5:21	Courtesy of Grant and Abie Beck Collection
7:24	Courtesy of Grant and Abie Beck Collection
7:25	Courtesy of Grant and Abie Beck Collection
8:26	Courtesy of Grant and Abie Beck Collection
8:29	Courtesy of Grant and Abie Beck Collection
9:30	Courtesy of Grant and Abie Beck Collection
9:32	Collection of the Jackson Hole Historical Society and Museum
10:36	Courtesy of Doris Platts Collection
10:39	Courtesy of Doris Platts Collection
10:40	Courtesy of Grant and Abie Beck Collection
10:45	Courtesy of Doris Platts Collection
10:47	Courtesy of Grant and Abie Beck Collection
11:48a	Collection of the Jackson Hole Historical Society and Museum
11:48b	Collection of the Jackson Hole Historical Society and Museum
11:51	Courtesy of Grant and Abie Beck Collection; Photograph by Scott Bjornson
12:52	Courtesy of Grant and Abie Beck Collection
12:54	Courtesy of Grant and Abie Beck Collection
12:57	Courtesy of Grant and Abie Beck Collection
13:58	Collection of the Jackson Hole Historical Society and Museum
13:61	Collection of the Jackson Hole Historical Society and Museum
14:65	Courtesy of Grant and Abie Beck Collection
15:66	Courtesy of Bill Bowlsby Collection
15:68	Courtesy of Bill Bowlsby Collection
15:71	Courtesy of Bill Bowlsby Collection
16:72	Courtesy of Sam Hair Collection
16:74	Courtesy of Grant and Abie Beck Collection
16:77	Courtesy of Doris Platts Collection
17:78	Courtesy of Chick Joy
17:80	Courtesy of Doris Platts Collection
17:81	Courtesy of Doris Platts Collection
17:82	Courtesy of Chick Joy
17:83	Courtesy of Chick Joy
18:84	Courtesy of Grant and Abie Beck Collection
18:86	Courtesy of Doris Platts Collection
19:88	Courtesy of Grant and Abie Beck Collection
19:93	Courtesy of Dan Abernathy
20:94	Courtesy of Grant and Abie Beck Collection

SOURCES OF PHOTOGRAPHS

20:96 Courtesy of Grant and Abie Beck Collection
21:99 Courtesy of Grant and Abie Beck Collection
22:101 Courtesy of Bob Sullivan Collection
22:104 Courtesy of Bob Sullivan Collection
23:105 Collection of the Jackson Hole Historical Society and Museum
23:109 Collection of the Jackson Hole Historical Society and Museum
24:110 Courtesy of Grant and Abie Beck Collection
24:113 Courtesy of Eldon Ross
25:114 Courtesy of Grant and Abie Beck Collection
25:117 Courtesy of Sam Hair Collection
26:118 Courtesy of Bob Sullivan Collection
26:120 Courtesy of Bob Sullivan Collection
26:123 Courtesy of Sam Hair Collection
27:124a Courtesy of Bob Sullivan Collection
27:124b Courtesy of Bob Sullivan Collection
28:128 Courtesy of Bob Sullivan Collection
28:130 Courtesy of Bob Sullivan Collection
28:131 Courtesy of Bob Sullivan Collection
29:133 Courtesy of Sam Hair Collection
30:134 Courtesy of Grant and Abie Beck Collection
31:138 Courtesy of Sam Hair Collection
31:139 Courtesy of Grant and Abie Beck Collection
32:140 Courtesy of Grant and Abie Beck Collection
33:144 Courtesy of Bob Sullivan Collection
33:146 Courtesy of Bob Sullivan Collection
34:150 Courtesy of Grant and Abie Beck Collection
34:151 Courtesy of Grant and Abie Beck Collection
34:153 Courtesy of Grant and Abie Beck Collection
35:154 Courtesy of Bob Sullivan Collection
35:158 Courtesy of Bob Sullivan Collection
35:160 Courtesy of Bob Sullivan Collection
36:162 Courtesy of Sam Hair Collection
37:164 Courtesy of Grant and Abie Beck Collection
37:166 Courtesy of Sam Hair Collection
38:170a Courtesy of Grant and Abie Beck Collection
38:170b Courtesy of Grant and Abie Beck Collection
38:171 Courtesy of Grant and Abie Beck Collection
39:172 Courtesy of Grant and Abie Beck Collection
40:176a Courtesy of Grant and Abie Beck Collection
40:176b Courtesy of Grant and Abie Beck Collection
40:176c Courtesy of Grant and Abie Beck Collection
40:176d Courtesy of Grant and Abie Beck Collection
41:180 Courtesy of Dr: William Close
41:185a Courtesy of Bob Sullivan Collection
41:185b Courtesy of Bob Sullivan Collection
42:186 Courtesy of Bob Sullivan Collection
42:188a Courtesy of the Jankiwiecz Family
42:188b Courtesy of the Jankiwiecz Family

ACKNOWLEDGMENTS

Grant Beck has touched so many people during his life it would not have been possible to tell his story properly without the help of a few of them. While Grant's personal stories are the backbone of the book, anecdotes shared first-hand by friends and acquaintances truly round it out. Thank you for conveying and sharing your experiences: Lee Gilbert, Leif Lie, Eldon Ross, Donna Sievers, Maureen Curley, Peter T. Tomaras, and Wes Miller.

The stories came to life with the accompaniment of photos graciously furnished by Doris Platts, the late Sam Hair, Dan Abernathy, William Bowlsby and Chick Joy. A special thanks to the staff for their assistance and for the source materials found at the Jackson County Historical Society, Jackson Hole, WY.

Where just the right photo could not be discovered, the illustrations by my good friend Dan Regan are a worthy and brilliant substitute. For his writing expertise and editorial guidance, a very sincere thanks to Pat DiNatale. No book comes to life without the careful selection and attention to detail of the right design and layout. *Camp Coffee* is no exception. A warm thank you for his generosity and the masterful work created to frame *Camp Coffee*'s text by my close friend and cohort Jeremy Ragonese as well as graphic artist Dusty Sumner for his design contributions including the book's cover.

Although Grant came first in my life, my wife Sally, and my two daughters Heather and Nicole, control the heart-strings. They too have had the good fortune of knowing Grant and being a part of the story. But it's Sally who has made possible all things meaningful in my life. In that same vein, as there is almost always a special woman behind each man's most significant contributions, Grant's stories would never have been told or this book ever printed without the support of his wife Abie.

I first met Abigail Dowd Beck when she came to the Two Bar Spear Ranch from Atlanta as a camp counselor almost 30 years ago. Since that time Abie has left a lasting impression on every one of the ranch's visitors through her caring and generosity. If you've had the opportunity to read *Enduring Women*, there is a striking resemblance to Harriett "Hickey" Johnston's life and her relationship to husband Charlie Johnston, with that of Grant and Abie's. Abie, thanks for helping make this project a reality.

BIBLIOGRAPHY

Abernathy, Dan 2000, 'To Know What You Want', *American Cowboy*, May/June, pp. 41-45.

Back, Joe & Lemmon, Vic 1986, *The Old Guide Remembers & the Young Guide Finds Out*, Johnson Books, Boulder, Colorado.

Beck, Abie, *Two Bar Spear Ranch Summer Camp* [Pamphlet] Pinedale, Wyoming.

Beck, Abie, *Two Bar Spear Ranch Pack Trips* [Pamphlet] Pinedale, Wyoming.

Belding, Cheryl E. 1993, *Twelfth Generation: +4382 i. Arthur William Bowlsby* [On-line] http://www.bowlbyfamily.org/ancestor/di7296.htm, 21 Dec. 2002.

Braban, Yasmin 1998. 'Grant Beck Celebrates 50 Years as an Outfitter', *Pinedale Roundup*, 24 September, p.11.

Curley, Maureen 2003, *Grant Beck* [Personal e-mail] 24 Jan. 2003.

Daugherty, John, 1999, *A Place Called Jackson Hole*, Moose, Wyoming: Grand Teton National Park.

Dirks, Tim 1996-2002. *Greatest Films: Shane (1953)* [On-line] http://www.filmsite.org, 25 Dec. 2002.

Gentry, Diane Koos 1988, *Enduring Women*, Texas A&M University Press, College Station, Texas.

Gilbert, Lee 2002, *Grant Beck* [Personal e-mail] 11 April, 2002.

Horton, Jon. *When I was a Kid We Had a Neighbor Named Banty Bowlsby* [On-line] http://www. jacksonholenet.com/column/westwyo/banty.htm, 12 Dec. 2002.

Hough, Donald 1956, *The Cocktail Hour in Jackson Hole*, The Vail-Ballou Press, Denver, Colorado; W. W. Norton & Company, Inc. New York.

Kent, Anne 1959, 'Fugitive from Justice Apprehended,' *Jackson's Hole Courier*, 11 June.

Platts, Doris 2002, *letter from Wilson*, Wyoming [Personal letter] 11 April.

Postman, Neil, *Time 100: Scientists & Thinkers – Philo Farnsworth* [On-line] http:/www.time.com/time/time100/scientist/profile/farnsworth, 26 Dec. 2002.

BIBLIOGRAPHY

Raine, Lee 2002. *Branding I.* Cowboy Showcase
[On-line] http://www.cowboyshowcase.com/brands.htm, 18 Jan. 2003.

Ross, Eldon 2001, *letter from Quartzite, Arizona* [Personal letter] 4 Feb.

Ruland, Tim 2004, 'The Subtle Legacy of Grant Beck and the Two Bar Spear Girl's Camp,' *Pinedale Roundup*, 7 October, pp. 1 & 17.

Sievers, Donna 2002, *letter from Lake Havasu City, Arizona* [Personal letter] 18 Feb.

Woodbury, Chuck 2000, *In Tiny Rigby, Idaho the Inventor of TV is Honored*
[On-line] http://www.outwestnewspaper.com/tv.html, 26 Dec. 2002.

'Sgt. Forney Leaves St. John's Hospital on Own Power' 1959, *Jackson's Hole Courier*, 18 June.

'Pleads Guilty in District Court' 1959, *Jackson's Hole Courier*, 23 July.

'Sheriff Emery Resigns in Surprise Move' 1959, *Jackson's Hole Courier*, 6 August.

The Miller Ranch: Stuart McKinley interviewing Mildred Miller
[On-line] http://www.grvm.com/brands/miller.htm, 18 Jan. 2003.

'Bowlsby was 95' 1993, *Jackson Hole Guide*, 28 April, p. B9.

'Log Cabin Bar Has New Owners' 1963, *Jackson's Hole Courier*, 10 October.

'Miss Anita Tarbell is Called to Death' 1960, *Jackson's Hole Courier*, 11 August.

The Log Cabin Club/Saloon. Jackson Hole Historical Society and Museum, 19 Sept. 2001.

The Saga of the Wort Hotel [On-line] http://www.worthotel.com/history_body.html, 4 Jan. 2003.

Half Moon Ranch for Girls 1930 [Pamphlet], Moose, Wyoming.

'Corporation of Half Moon Ranch' 1928, *Jackson's Hole Courier*, Nov.

"Horsepacking' 1979, *Signals*, Jan. pp 8-12.

ABOUT THE AUTHOR

For about as long as he can remember, Kansas City, MO, native Bob Sullivan dreamed of being a cowboy. Not until an abrupt disillusionment with college athletics in 1975 did he drop out of school and move to Wyoming to pursue his dream. He was 19 years old.

Meeting and working for Grant Beck at the Two Bar Spear Ranch in Pinedale, WY, had a lasting impact on the author's life. His experiences in Wyoming, and subsequent relationship with Grant over the next 30 years, inspired Bob to share Grant's remarkable life with others.

While home for Christmas in 1976, a chance introduction to Sally Haertling, the future Mrs. Sally Sullivan, brought him back to Kansas City. Bob had been back from Wyoming three years when he tried to transfer some of the ranch skills he had learned to the rodeo arena. After being knocked unconscious after only his second ride on a saddle bronc in the Kansas City Rodeo, Sally encouraged him to find a different horse outlet.

During a nine-year tenure in the Denver, CO, area the Sullivans raised and showed Quarter Horses and Appaloosas. Following a three-year stint in Chicago, Bob and family returned to Kansas City in 1994. They consider themselves fortunate to share their current home with a half-dozen of their four-hoofed friends. Three years ago Bob crossed another one of his goals off the list when, with the help of 20-year PRCA rodeo veteran and friend Phil Haugen, he purchased his first heeling horse, Jessie, and began team roping.

Camp Coffee is the author's second book. Interestingly, it was riding not writing that inspired him to ever pick up a pen. "As with most people, in most instances, a good horse will bring out the best in all of us."

Grant Beck bringing up the rear on Jackie down the trail by Nell Lake. *Photo courtesy of Sam Hair.*